Gothic jewelry

35 SCARY PROJECTS TO MAKE, GIVE, AND WEAR

Harriet Smith

CICO BOOKS
LONDON NEW YORK

I would like to dedicate this book to Anne and Paul Smith,
my incredibly supportive parents.

Published in 2011 by CICO Books
An imprint of Ryland Peters & Small Ltd

20–21 Jockey's Fields   519 Broadway, 5th Floor
London WC1R 4BW   New York, NY 10012

www.cicobooks.com

10 9 8 7 6 5 4 3 2 1

Text © Harriet Smith 2011
Design and photography © CICO Books 2011

A CIP catalog record for this book is available from the Library
of Congress and the British Library.

ISBN: 978 1 907563 82 9

Printed in China

Editor: Marie Clayton
Designer: Luis Peral-Aranda
Photographer: Martin Norris
Styling and Photographic Art Direction: Luis Peral-Aranda

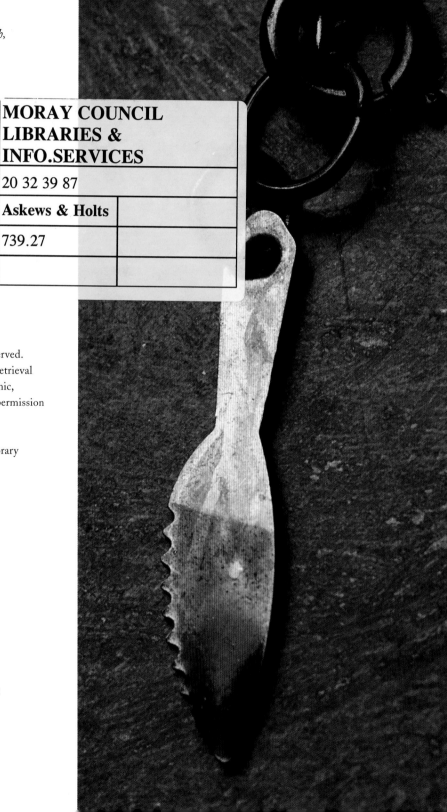

CONTENTS

INTRODUCTION

The experience of writing this book has been thoroughly rewarding and a great compliment for a new graduate—I studied jewelry design for three years at Central Saint Martins, part of the University of the Arts London, graduating in summer 2010. The Gothic theme and horror styling was a mindset easily adopted—I'm drawn to anything gory, so the more blood and guts the better as far as I'm concerned! My major degree collection was inspired by horror cinema and the stimulation of fear: namely by Madagascan Giant Hissing Cockroaches (I had a tank full in my room). The roaches were my own movie monsters and homage to my love of Hammer Horror's lack of subtlety and tongue-in-cheek humor.

Everything associated with horror intrigues me: from iconic 1950s movie artwork to shamelessly lowbrow slasher films. I love extremes and the adrenaline rush from being scared; it's great fun with a little shock and controversy combined. There's nothing really gory in this book but I hope I've captured the comedy horror vibe I set out to recreate. If you sympathize with this style, try making the Amber Spider Necklace on page 118—you just need to find some bugs of your own to "preserve." If you're more into Bram Stoker and the classical Gothic aesthetic, the Velvet Skull Choker (page 40) or the Gothic Cross Necklace (page 92) could be designs to inspire you. These projects made me reminisce about a trip I made to Transylvania a few years ago, exploring the Carpathian Mountains, absorbing the eerie charm of the Gothic architecture (and generally avoiding bears).

Creating these pieces required visits to my favorite materials supply haunts around London, which I have listed in the back of the book along with new outlets found through the Internet. Most projects are flexible on material variations, so feel free to adapt designs to suit your personal style or budget limitations. I like to experiment with unusual materials and use objects not intended for jewelry production. My design process generally starts with testing different material combinations and then considering how they could sympathetically adorn the body; for instance the Bottle Top Cameo Bracelet (page 114) and matching ring and earrings utilize discarded soda/beer tops.

The first chapter of this book covers the materials, tools, and techniques used most frequently. I have chosen equipment that is inexpensive and which you are certain to use time and again. No soldering is involved in any projects; primarily because my workshop is literally my bedroom—I tell you this to illustrate the approachability of the work involved to produce the jewelry! Essentially, all you need is a clear work surface.

Have fun, be innovative, and try something new—you will get a real satisfaction from making and wearing something unique instead of the usual high-street mass-produced designs.

Harriet Smith

London, 2011

TOOLS & BASIC TECHNIQUES

This first chapter covers the tools, materials, and techniques I use most frequently in the projects. It also includes many handy tips and shortcuts, which will make life easier as you work. There are a number of projects based on using resin or acrylic sheet and some that require basic sheet metalwork, but no soldering is involved.

TOOLS

You probably own most of the basic tools already, although there might be a few new additions required for your toolbox. I have chosen the most useful and inexpensive items that you're certain to use time and again.

Pliers

A good assortment of pliers will be invaluable for most jewelry-making techniques. You do not have to buy every type shown here at once; start with a couple of pairs of flat-nose pliers and a pair of round-nose pliers and buy others as and when you need them.

Round-nose pliers
These have round jaws and are used to create loops and rings in wire, such as when making eye loops. The jaws are tapered so you can make different-sized loops.

Needle-nose pliers
The long narrow jaws on these pliers are used to hold small items and manipulate wire, and may have a cutting edge to cut wire. They are also known as chain-nose pliers.

Bail-making pliers
With one flat and one domed jaw, these pliers are used to create bigger loops and rings in wire, and to create decorative bails.

Flat-nose pliers
Used to open and close jump rings without deforming their shape—you will need two pairs for this. The square jaws are also useful to create sharp angles in wire or thin sheet.

Parallel pliers
Adjustable pliers with jaws that move parallel to each other so they grip evenly along their length, which means they can be used to hold items securely.

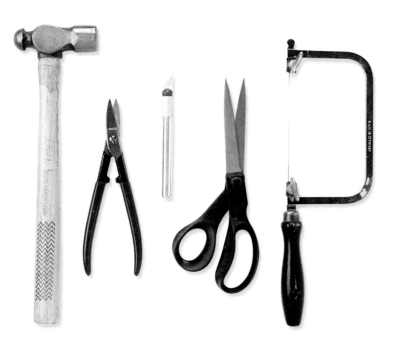

Cutting and shaping tools (left)

Ball pein hammer
A fairly heavyweight hammer with one flat end and one ball end, used to flatten metal, set rivets, and create textures on the metal surface.

Wire snips
These can be used to cut both wire and thin metal sheet. They usually cut the wire end into a point—so if you need a flat cut end, use flush cutters instead.

Craft knife
Handy for cutting out Fimo® pieces before final shaping. They can also be used to cut lightweight sheet materials or trim excess resin.

Fabric scissors
These are used to cut fabric, ribbon, and cord. Keep the blades sharp and do not use them to cut paper, since this will blunt them quickly.

Piercing saw
Similar to a small hacksaw, this is used to cut shapes from sheet metal. The blade can be unfastened and inserted through a drilled hole to cut out internal shapes. Blades vary according to their tooth size: 2.0 is a fairly versatile and strong choice for cutting most sheet metals.

Clamps and vices (right)

Tweezers
Tweezers are useful to hold and position very small components, especially crystals; the type with pointed tips are better than the flat-tipped type for accuracy.

Vice with bench block
A small vice can be clamped onto a table or bench to hold small items securely. This one includes a bench block (flat area to left of jaws) as a firm, flat base for hammering.

Bench pin
Simply a sheet of wood with a V-shape cut out: you could easily make your own. This needs to be clamped to your work surface: it is useful to support small objects when sawing or filing.

Line the jaws of the vice with cork or foam to avoid marking delicate items. The vice pictured has a small built-in bench block, which is all you need for the projects in this book.

The bench pin is clamped to the edge of your work surface; the cut-out shape at the front makes it easier to saw and file small items.

Power and heating tools

The multi-tool is ideal for jewelry making and has a good selection of bits and sanding and polishing heads that will save you time. However, if you don't have one you can use a small drill for making holes and file or sand by hand.

Heat gun
This hand-held device blows very hot air that will heat and soften acrylic sheet ready for shaping. It is available from most craft and hobby stores.

Multi-tool plus drill bits and heads
Multi-tools have an assortment of drills and interchangeable heads, so you can use them for fast drilling, sanding, and polishing.

Lighter
An ordinary cigarette lighter is useful for singeing the edges of fabric for an authentic distressed look.

Finishing and polishing tools

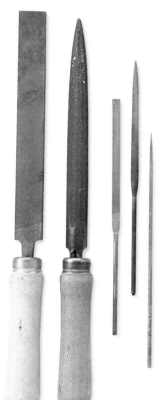

Files (assorted for metal and plastic)
Files come in different sizes and shapes and are used to smooth the edges of sawn metal or acrylic. The flat hand file and the half round file are useful for larger areas, while for detailed work use smaller needle files.

Clay modeling tools
These are available in assorted shapes and are typically plastic or wooden with a mixture of straight, pointed, and rounded edges. They are used to shape and model material such as Fimo®.

Polishing cloth
A soft cloth for applying a final shine to metal or plastic. It can be used alone, or with a suitable polishing agent such as metal polish.

Emery or wet-and-dry paper
Available in several grades: 150 grit is coarse, while 2000 grit is fine. Wet-and-dry paper can be used with water for gentle abrasion and a smoother finish; it is ideal for use with plastics, especially.

Burnisher
A hardened steel tool that is rubbed firmly over already filed and sanded metal to add a final shine.

You should have a different set of files for metal and for plastic to maintain their efficiency.

You can use emery paper by hand, or attach it to a length of wood using double-sided tape to act as a straight, directional file.

Brass brush
The metal bristles of this brush are used for cleaning up metal or adding polished highlights to areas with a patina finish.

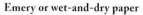

Other tools

Rolling pin
Wooden rolling pin to roll out Fimo® to a smooth sheet of a regular thickness, ready to cut out the required shape.

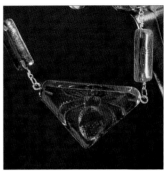

Molds for resin
The special molds available for resin casting usually have pairs of shapes, as shown here. You can also use any small mold designed for baking.

Measuring spoons for resin
Measuring spoons are more accurate for small quantities; for larger quantities, a small measuring jug may be more useful.

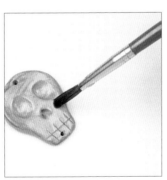

Paintbrush
Choose a paintbrush with bristles that taper to a point, which will be more useful for detail work.

Ruler
A ruler marked in both metric and imperial measurements is ideal. A metal type will also be handy to use as a guide when using a craft knife.

Marker pen
Permanent markers that will write on a variety of materials are the best option. Any marks left at the end can usually be sanded away.

Molds specifically for resin casting are available from modeling shops and online, or you can use flexible plastic molds and silicone molds designed for baking.

Safety equipment

Goggles
This type of goggles will protect your eyes from fine dust or flying chips when cutting and filing.

Gloves
The gloves shown here are a heat-protective type for use when shaping hot acrylic sheet. Thin latex gloves will also be useful when dealing with chemicals such as liver of sulfur and when mixing and pouring resin.

Dust mask
Simple dust masks like this are readily available at craft and hobby stores, so keep a good supply to hand.

Wear a dust mask and goggles when filing plastics, in particular—the fine dust is dangerous if breathed in.

Latex gloves not only protect your hands when using chemicals, but will also prevent your greasy fingerprints from causing uneven smudges when you are dipping items in liver of sulfur.

Work in a well-ventilated area when mixing and pouring resin.

MATERIALS

Most of the materials I have used in the projects are readily available from craft shops or hobby stores. In some cases I have suggested alternative materials so you have one or more options—don't be afraid to experiment with what is available.

Findings

There is a vast array of ready-made findings available in most bead shops and the variations are endless. I have used various styles that I thought worked best in the designs, but you can interchange the styles as you prefer and according to what you can find.

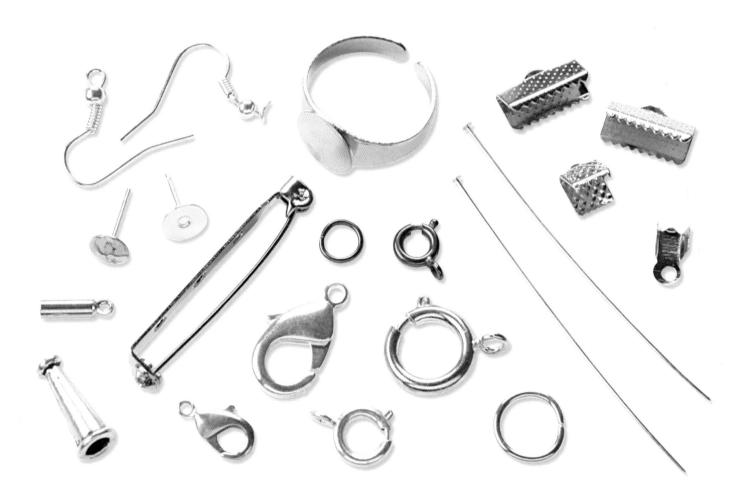

*Ready-made Fimo®
flower beads and bells were
good finds and Swarovski
HotFix crystals are great for
incorporating in the Fimo®.*

*You can also buy items not
intended for use in jewelry
making and reinvent their
purpose. In this book I use a
few things from joke/magic
shops, such as imitation blood
and plastic spiders.*

Beads, crystals, and found objects

Bead stores stock a comprehensive range of beads and crystals, and
these are also available online. Plastic or crystal beads and flat-backed
(cabochon) stones are inexpensive, but the price is much higher for
glass—particularly Swarovski crystals, although if you only have a couple
in the design it's worth paying more for the extra sparkle.

Modeling and molding materials

There are many different options for modeling and molding, but these are the materials that I have used in the projects. From left to right in the photograph: Siligum 2-part silicone mold-making putty, resin with hardener to the left and pigment to the right, blocks of Fimo®, and cylinders of Milliput.

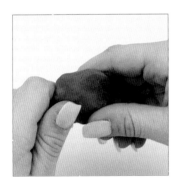

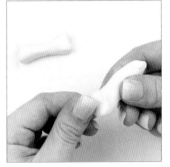

Fimo® only hardens on baking, so there are no time constraints on the modeling process. You can get a vast array of colors as well as some special effect finishes—on the Insects Web Necklace (page 52) I used a glow-in-the dark version. The hardened clay can be drilled and Fimo® brand gloss varnish can be applied to give a great shine.

Milliput® 2-part epoxy putty is a UK product that is available worldwide online. I use Superfine White, which is largely sold for ceramic repair, because I like the quality of its smooth finish. It dries relatively quickly, but adding small amounts of water will keep it workable during modeling. Once fully hardened it can be drilled, filed, and sanded very smooth. Drying time is around two hours. Any similar epoxy putty or epoxy clay designed for modeling or ceramic repair will do as an alternative.

Siligum 2-part silicone mold-making putty is also a UK product, but is available online. It is very usable as it comes in solid form and can be manipulated by hand. Almost any hard object can be pressed into it to make a copy. The hardening time is within minutes and you can produce over 50 casts in crystal resin or polymer clay per mold. As an alternative, you could try Contenti Cold Mold Compound, or similar.

EnviroTex Lite® pouring resin is probably the most environmentally friendly choice of casting resins available. Pigments to color it are sold in many colors and are mostly available in both translucent and opaque types; you can also combine colors to make your own shades.

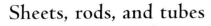

Sheets, rods, and tubes

These are available in many different materials, so you can choose what will look best in your project. From left to right in the photograph: brass rod and tube, walnut square rod, walnut, copper, aluminum, and acrylic sheet.

Sheet metal can be purchased in a range of different thicknesses—I have mostly used around 5mm upward, which is relatively easy to cut for those unfamiliar with using a piercing saw but rigid enough to hold a cut shape. **Base metal sheet** can be found in good hardware and model-making stores, while **silver sheet** can be bought in jewelry specialist shops or online in any quantity.

Beading and craft shops stock a range of **wires**—it is up to your budget whether you opt for silver or copper/brass. Wire also comes in different sizes—I use 0.3mm silver-plated wire for fine beadwork, 0.6mm for small forms that require detailed forming, and 0.8mm or 1.2mm for larger structures and jump rings with stems (anything that must keep its shape or support weight).

I have used 3mm **Perspex®** for the acrylic sheet projects in the book, which you can find in pretty much any color imaginable. It's inexpensive to buy and available from many art and modeling shops or online. **Plexiglas®** is a similar product that is available worldwide.

Walnut sheet/square rod can be purchased from modeling supply shops. Other varieties of wood are fine as an alternative, as long as they are not too soft—if necessary, you can alter the color easily with wood stain. The sheet comes in various thicknesses and the square rod is ideal for making crosses. You can cut the wood with a piercing saw and file/sand the edges smooth by hand or with a multi-tool.

Fabric and stringing materials

Many stringing materials can be found in sewing supply and bead stores. More unusual choices, such as craft leaves and feathers, can be sourced in specialist trade shops or online. Stringing cords are often a cheaper alternative to chain and if you find one you particularly like, buying a reel to cut from as required will save you money.

Other materials

Epoxy adhesive

This 2-part adhesive is readily available and is used to achieve high-strength bonds. Different types have different setting times, so always follow the instructions. The glue will dry clear and any small amounts of excess can be removed with acetone (nail polish remover).

Superglue

This glue offers an almost instant bond, but may not be successful at bonding some material combinations together.

Spray and enamel paint

Choose the correct type of paint for the material, because coverage and quality of finish will be better. Cover adjacent areas with masking tape when using spray paint and apply coats in thin layers.

Liver of sulfur

This chemical is mixed with water and used to add patina to metal. The hotter and stronger the solution, the quicker it will turn metal to gunmetal color. There are a number of alternative chemicals that will oxidize different metal types: liver of sulfur is most effective when used on silver and copper.

Renaissance wax

A microcrystalline wax coating that can be applied to metal to preserve the finish and protect it from contamination.

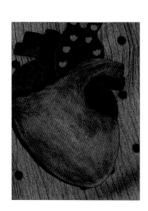

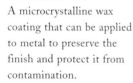

TECHNIQUES

The following techniques are used again and again in various projects throughout the book, so they are explained here in detail. The project instructions have cross-referencing back to these pages as a reminder.

Opening and closing jump rings

 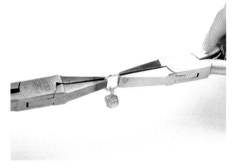

I Hold the jump ring with flat-nose pliers, one pair on either side of the join. Twist the pliers away from one another, so the ends of the jump ring separate but stay in alignment.

2 Add the item to the jump ring as required, or thread it on to use as a connection. To close, use the pliers again to twist the ends back toward each other to meet neatly. This avoids distorting the shape of the ring.

In some projects I have used thinner wire for the wire eye loop and then wrapped the end around the stem to finish, rather than snipping it off (see Making a dangle, opposite). This adds an extra bit of detailing.

Forming a wire eye loop

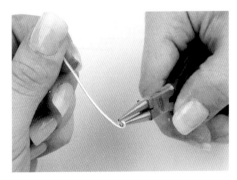 

I Bend the end of the wire around into a circular loop of the size you require, using round-nose pliers.

2 Grip the base of the loop with the pliers and bend it back slightly, so the eye sits over the center of the wire. Cut the wire stem to the required length.

Adding a catch and extension chain

1 Use a jump ring to join one half of the catch to the end of a chain, or you can add the catch to an end eye loop.

2 You can also add an extension chain to the other side of the item, so the length can be adjusted as required.

Making a dangle

1 Take a head pin, eye pin, or length of wire and thread on your selected bead or charm. Use the round-nose pliers to loop the other end of the wire around.

2 Center the loop over the bead and either twist the wire end around itself to finish off, or cut off the excess wire.

You can thread on more than one bead to make longer dangles.

If you thread the beads or a suitable charm with an eye loop at each end, you can use this as a decorative link to create a rosary chain for a bracelet or necklace.

Using a piercing saw

 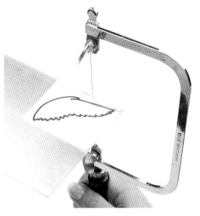 

1 Undo the screws on each slot of the saw. Insert the end of the blade into the bottom slot and tighten the screw. Press the top of the saw firmly downward, at the same time inserting the other end of the saw blade and tightening the screw. The saw will spring back slightly when the downward pressure is released, so the blade will be taut.

2 Mark out the shape you want to cut. To make the first cut, draw the blade down from the bottom of the blade to the top and then slide back up again. Repeat this motion cutting on the down stroke each time, making sure you keep the blade straight and untangled.

3 To cut an internal shape, drill a hole large enough to take the saw blade within the area to be removed. Unscrew one end of the blade, insert it through the drilled hole, and then tighten again, as described in step 1. Cut the shape as in step 2. Unscrew the blade to remove it from the shape.

Filing

 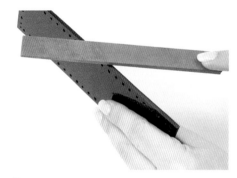 

1 After you have cut any shape from metal, file the edges carefully to smooth out any irregularities. A multi-tool fitted with a grinding head will remove material quickly; use needle files for detail areas.

2 When filing acrylic sheet work in one direction only, following the marks on the plastic edge and gradually working them away.

3 For the smoothest edge when filing acrylic sheet or other plastics, finish by using wet-and-dry emery paper with a little water.

When you are setting the saw blade in the saw, make sure that the teeth are on the outside and angled downward from the top of the saw.

When the blade is correctly inserted and taut, it will "ping" when plucked.

Drilling holes

I Mark the hole to be drilled beforehand— you could use a center punch or scribe, which will locate the drill bit accurately before you begin drilling. Make sure you keep the drill straight and perpendicular to the surface while you are drilling.

Making rivets

When using emery or sandpaper, work up through the grades from coarse to finer.

A little metal polish on a soft polishing cloth will add a final bright shine to the cut edges of acrylic sheet.

Be careful to avoid scratching the top and bottom surfaces of the acrylic sheet as you file the edges, because it will be impossible to remove any unwanted marks satisfactorily.

I Drill a hole to match the rod/tube to be riveted—the tighter the fit, the easier it will be to set the rivet. Thread the rod/tube through the drilled hole and cut it down so there is an equal amount protruding on either side (around ¹⁄₄in/0.5mm is adequate). Position on a bench block and use a hammer to tap the rod/tube ends gently until they spread. Turn over when secure and use the hammer on the other side to ensure a flush finish on each side.

Always make sure small items are held securely in a vice before you begin to drill into them. Very small items can be held with parallel pliers.

Use a soft metal, such as brass or copper, when making a "rivet" because it will be much easier to get the metal to spread evenly to achieve the correct riveted look.

Don't tap too hard when making rivets or you may damage the piece you are working on.

Using liver of sulfur

Silver and copper can be oxidized black by dipping in a solution of liver of sulfur. Prepare half a cup of hot (not boiling) water and add about 10 drops of liquid liver of sulfur. Clean the metal to be oxidized with liquid soap to degrease the surface—avoid touching it with your fingertips afterwards or wear latex gloves. Drop the part into the liver of sulfur solution, using tweezers to pick it out again; it will take less than 10 seconds to color.

Work in a well-ventilated area, as the liver of sulfur solution has a gross rotten-egg stink.

To achieve a darker result, build the color in layers by dunking then washing the part multiple times; if you just leave it for longer in the solution the oxidization will chip off later.

For a brushed gray or caviar coloration instead of black, try going over the oxidized metal very gently with a brass brush.

Brass brushing

1 Brush gently with a brass brush, either to create a satin finish on a shiny surface or to remove some patina for extra contrast in parts of the design.

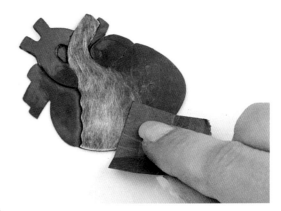

2 You can also rub across the surface gently with coarse emery paper for a similar effect. Try different grades for different finishes.

Making a mold

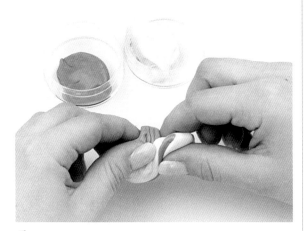

1 Take equal amounts of silicone molding paste and hardener—which are usually different colors—and knead them together until the mix is an even color all through.

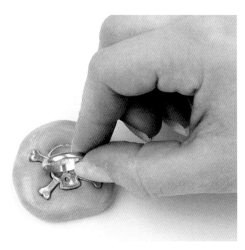

2 Take the small item to mold and press it firmly into the molding putty to take an impression. Leave the mold to harden—this takes around 5–10 minutes—then remove the item so the mold is ready to use.

Mixing and pouring casting resin

Whichever brand of casting resin you opt for, follow the manufacturer's guidelines on mixing—most resins are 2-part and need to be combined in specific quantities. You will need measuring equipment such as baking measure spoons or cups with ml markings. After pouring the mixed resin into the mold, leave to harden for the recommended time.

Various pigments are available to add color to resin, in both translucent and opaque. Pigment should be added during the mixing process, after you have added the catalyst, and stirred in well so that it spreads evenly through the mix.

Always pour resin and leave it to cure in a well-ventilated area: outside in the fresh air is the best option, weather permitting.

After removing the shape from the mold, remove any rough edges or excess resin that has seeped out with a fine file or wet-and-dry emery paper.

If pouring resin into a tight or awkward mold, using a little mold release spray before pouring is advisable.

Molding Fimo® into flat shapes

 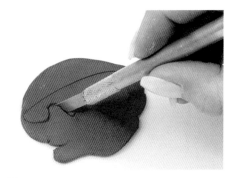 

1 Start by kneading the block of Fimo® to soften it, so it will be easier to shape. To make a flat shape, roll it out to the thickness required using a rolling pin.

2 Cut out the shape required, using a sharp craft knife; for complex shapes, you could draw the outline gently into the surface first.

3 Smooth and refine the edges of the shape as required, using a modeling tool. Place the parts on a flat baking tray and bake according to the manufacturer's instructions and your oven specifications. Allow to cool and harden before drilling or varnishing.

Molding Fimo® into 3-D shapes

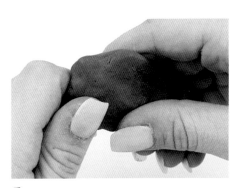 

1 After kneading the Fimo® to warm and soften it as before, begin to shape it roughly with your fingers. Fimo® Soft is easier to work for beginners, but Fimo® Classic provides a more durable finished result.

2 Continue refining the shape with the tips of your fingers—you can use a modeling tool to add extra detail if required. Place the parts on a flat baking tray and bake according to the manufacturer's instructions and your oven specifications. Allow to cool and harden before drilling or varnishing.

You can mix Fimo® colors together completely to create new colors, or only partly to create a marbled effect. Separate parts can simply be pushed together—they will fix on baking.

It is essential that your work surface is clean, dry, and free of any particles that could be picked up in the clay.

Using a heat gun to form acrylic sheet

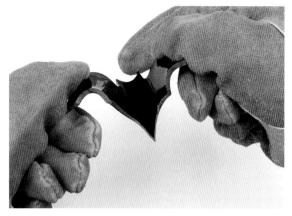

1 File and sand the acrylic edges until all the marks are smoothed out, as explained on page 24. Remove the protective coverings from both sides of the acrylic sheet. Using a heat gun, apply even heat over the whole shape until the acrylic becomes soft and flexible.

2 Wearing thick protective gloves to protect your hands, shape the acrylic sheet into the form you need while it is still hot. Hold in place to maintain the shape until the acrylic has cooled and set.

Do not overheat the acrylic with the heat gun, because the surface will begin to bubble and spoil. Apply heat gradually until the piece is soft enough to shape.

To cool and set the acrylic shape quickly, quench it under cold running water.

Heat forming acrylic sheet to create a perfectly symmetrical form is difficult and will probably take a few attempts. Rather than continuously trying to shape it, allow the acrylic to cool and then slowly heat it up again to adapt isolated areas.

Lark's head knot

1 Fold the length of ribbon or cord in half, and then thread the central loop through whatever the ribbon or cord is to be fixed onto.

2 Thread the two ends of ribbon or cord through the central loop and pull to tighten the knot.

Slipknot

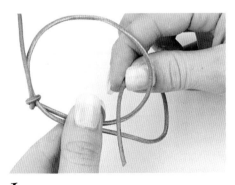  

1 Overlap the two ends of the pieces of cord by around 2in (5cm). Hold around 1in (2.5cm) of overlap together, one above the other. Take one end of the upper cord round and up through the circle.

2 Take the end of the cord over and round and thread it up through the circle again, this time taking it through the loop of the knot you are making.

3 Pull on the end to tighten the knot. Repeat with the other cord end. Both knots should be able to slide freely so that the wearer can adapt the size of the item.

Adding a crimp end

I Cut off any fraying at the end of the ribbon or cord. Hold a suitable crimp end in the pliers and slide the end of the ribbon or cord into the jaws. Squeeze the pliers to close the crimp end securely onto the ribbon or cord, but do not apply too much pressure or you will press the crimp end out of shape.

Using a crimp bead

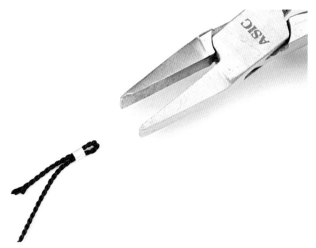

I To make an end loop in cord, thread the cord through a crimp bead and then double it over and thread it back through again. Squash the crimp bead evenly with the pliers so that it grips the cord tightly. Cut off any excess cord end close to the crimp bead.

If you only want to prevent the end from fraying, seal synthetic cord or ribbon with a lighter flame and dip into a little superglue.

If the ribbon or silk cord is kinked, the steam from a boiling kettle will straighten it out.

CHAPTER 2

FABRIC, MOLDING, & MODELING

The fabric pieces in this book are quite simple to construct using only basic hand stitching—I'm by no means an accomplished stitcher myself. Using Fimo® and epoxy putty is an immediate way to create unique and colorful 3-D forms, which can be incorporated into jewelry easily by drilling and attaching findings.

BLEEDING BROOCH

*T*his brooch could be worn on a dark jacket for dramatic effect or even attached to a bag. A large kilt pin conveniently holds a shower of cartoon blood—the Fimo® blood drips are simple to form by hand and a glossy varnish finish gives them a "wet" appearance.

YOU WILL NEED
Materials: Red Fimo®, Fimo® gloss varnish, 40in (100cm) chain, kilt pin with attached loops, small and large jump rings, epoxy adhesive
Tools: *Rolling pin, craft knife, pin, paintbrush, 2 pairs of flat-nose pliers*
Extra: *Fimo® or clay modeling tools*

1 Roll out a thick sheet of red Fimo® and use a craft knife to cut the main dripping outline freehand. Work on the edges to soften the curves, continuing them smoothly onto the clay surface. Cut a groove into the back surface of the piece along the top edge, where the pin will be positioned.

2 For individual drips, create different-sized balls in red Fimo® and work by hand into irregular drip shapes. Make up to eight drips and pierce each one through the top with a pin. Bake all the Fimo® parts in the oven, following the manufacturer's instructions. Once cool, all the pieces can be painted with gloss varnish.

3 Hang the length of chain from the kilt pin. The chain should be kept as one length; to create the drapes use the smaller jump rings to connect it at intervals through the kilt pin loops. Cross the drapes over in a random way to make the design more interesting.

4 Add the larger jump rings to some of the individual blood drips and hang each one from the base of one of the chain drapes. Keep a couple of the large drips for the pin itself—attach these near the end of the pin, as shown in the photograph.

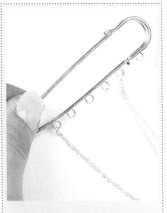

Look out for a large kilt pin with loop rings already fixed along one side. Often these pins are sold without and this will make attaching the blood splatter more awkward as the jump rings holding the chain will get in the way.

5 Fill the groove cut in the back of the main blood splatter in step 1 with lots of epoxy adhesive. Carefully position the pin in the groove and apply pressure to ensure firm contact. Position the piece to provide support as the adhesive dries.

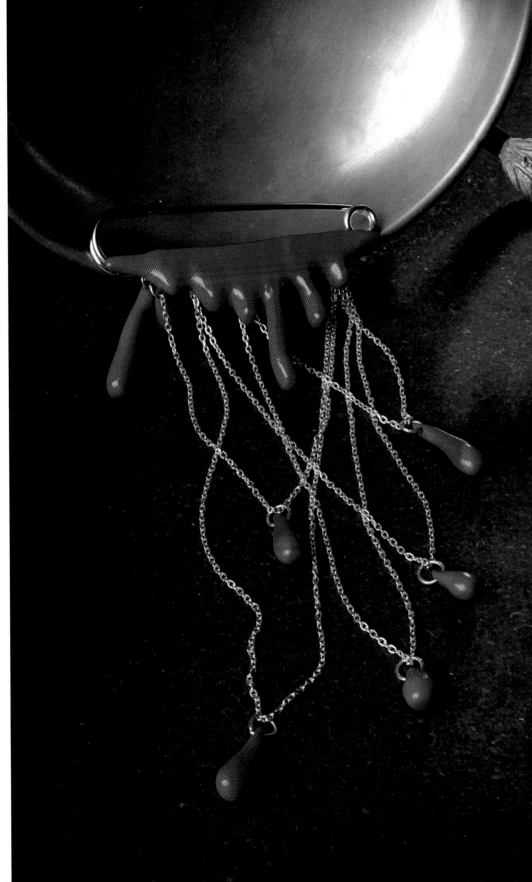

SKULL DANGLY EARRINGS

Quick and straightforward to make and all the materials can be found in a bead shop or art store. The skulls are made by hand in your choice of Fimo® color— black/gray/white works well and the size could be adjusted to suit your wearing comfort or style. The wooden beads are from a haberdashery shop.

YOU WILL NEED

Materials: *Fimo® in your choice of colors, 20-gauge (0.8mm) silver-plated wire or eye pins, 6 matching beads, 2 ear wires, varnish, jump rings*
Tools: *Wire snips, round-nose pliers, 2 pairs of flat-nose pliers*
Extra: *Fimo® or clay modeling tools*

1 Mold a piece of Fimo® by hand to construct the skull form—use modeling tools or the end of a pen/file to define the facial features. Make four skulls, two large and two small, then use wire to poke a small hole for hanging right through the top of each skull and through the bottom only of the larger skulls. Bake the Fimo® to harden, following the manufacturer's instructions.

2 Cut a length of wire and create an eye loop (see page 22) at one end, or use an eye pin. Thread three beads onto the wire. Create another eye loop at the other end and thread this into the base of an ear wire before closing.

3 Apply gloss varnish to each of the hardened skulls for a shiny finish. Add further coats of varnish if required, allowing each coat to dry thoroughly before applying the next.

4 Use jump rings to add the larger skull to the eye loop at the base of the beads, and to add the smaller skull to the bottom of the larger one. Repeat steps 2 through 4 to make the other earring.

WINGED HEART PENDANT

*T*his pendant catches the light with its unique crystal surface pattern made using Swarovski HotFix crystals, which eliminates awkward and messy gluing on the heart. The wings are bought beads but you can easily make them in Fimo® or use wings as a found object from a child's toy as an alternative.

YOU WILL NEED
Materials: 2 wing beads, 20-gauge (0.8mm) black oxidized wire, red Fimo®, Swarovski HotFix flat-backed crystals, epoxy adhesive, Fimo® gloss varnish, ribbon
Tools: Round- and flat-nose pliers, wire snips, tweezers, paintbrush, fabric scissors
Extra: Fimo® or clay modeling tools

1 Use pliers to make a U-shaped bail in twisted wire to hang the pendant. If the wings are modeled or are found objects, make a hole near the base. Make a wire eye loop (see page 22), threading the wire stem through the hole in each wing bead and then wrapping the end tightly back around the stem to secure.

2 Make the Fimo® heart by molding the form by hand (see page 28), using your fingers or modeling tools to smooth the edges and define the curves. Position the wings on either side near the top and push the wire eye loops into the clay to make anchor holes. Push the bail into the top of the heart in the same way.

3 Decorate the front of the heart with HotFix crystals, applied with tweezers using gentle pressure. You can add as many or as few as you wish. Carefully remove the wings and bail and bake the Fimo® following the manufacturer's instructions—the crystals will stick firmly as the glue on the back heats up.

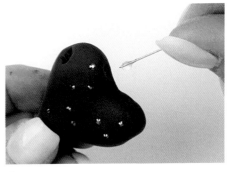

4 Once the heart is cool and hardened, insert epoxy adhesive into the bail and wing holes. Anchor the parts on firmly using plenty of adhesive, especially for the wings. Once the adhesive is dry, carefully paint the Fimo® heart with gloss varnish and allow to dry for the recommended time.

5 Cut a suitable length of ribbon for the length of pendant you want and secure through the heart bail with a simple lark's head knot (see page 30). Knot the other ends of the ribbon together with a double knot and trim the edges diagonally.

VELVET SKULL CHOKER

*O*ne of the more classically gothic pieces in the book, this piece is designed to be a choker, so adding an extension chain to the back is a good idea to accommodate different fit requirements.

YOU WILL NEED

Materials: *Skull item to mold, 2-part silicone mold-making putty, casting resin and pigment, velvet/lace ribbon trim, 2 crimp ends, catch, extension chain, jump rings, 2 small pearl beads, 2 head pins, 1 heart bead*

Tools: *Measuring cups for resin, fabric scissors, 2 pairs of flat-nose pliers, drill/multi-tool, wire snips*

I Take the small skull item you intend to mold and use a piece of mold putty (see page 27) to take an impression. Once the mold has fully hardened, carefully remove the skull item.

2 Mix the casting resin according to manufacturer's guidelines and add your chosen pigment color (see page 27). Pour the resin into the skull mold and then set aside to cure for the recommended time.

3 Cut a length of velvet/lace ribbon trim to around 12in (30cm) or to fit the wearer's neck. Add crimp ends to each end of the ribbon, using flat-nose pliers to pinch the ends closed (see page 31).

4 Add the catch and the extension chain to the crimp ends, using jump rings (see page 23). With the resin skull held in a vice, drill it three times, once through each eye socket and once through the mouth.

5 Thread the pearl beads onto head pins and thread these through the eye socket holes. Position the skull centrally on the ribbon, pushing the head pins through the ribbon. At the back, fold the ends of the head pins over in opposite directions to secure the skull in place and snip away any excess wire stem.

6 Add a jump ring to the top of the heart bead (see page 22) and then another jump ring to the first. Thread a third jump ring through the skull mouth and add the heart bead dangle to this, so it hangs from the base of the skull.

DEAD FLOWER CORSAGE

A traditionally gothic-styled accessory, this brooch combines different fabrics to give a layered petal effect. You don't need any real sewing skills to produce it (I certainly didn't!), just a few basic stitches to hold the petals in place and lots of glue. The large Swarovski crystal center could be in any of your favorite colors—everything will stand out against the black lace.

YOU WILL NEED
Materials: *Black lace, black lightweight fabric, fabric leaves, dark denim, brooch finding, epoxy adhesive, large colored crystal or stone*
Tools: *Fabric scissors, ruler, lighter or safety matches, needle and black thread*

1 Fold the lace over twice to create four layers. Cut through all the layers using sharp fabric scissors to make four circles, each around 4½in (11cm) in diameter.

2 Repeat step 1 to cut four slightly larger circles from black fabric. Use a lighter or matches to singe the edges of the fabric circles and of the ready-made fabric leaves.

3 Place a lace circle flat with a fabric circle on top and fold the double layer over into a semicircle and then again into a quadrant. Stitch into the corner to secure the layers in place. Repeat for the other three petals.

4 Cut two squares from black fabric and one from the lace, each measuring about 5 x 5in (12.5 x 12.5cm). Fold each square in half and then in half again the other way, to make a square of four layers. Cut around the raw edges only in a curve to create a petal shape. Unfold the square into a petal head.

5 Cut two circles each around 2in (5cm) in diameter out of the piece of dark denim—they don't need to be perfectly round. Cut one strip from the same denim that is slightly shorter than the diameter of the denim circles and around ½in (1cm) wide.

6 Position the four folded petals made in step 3 around one of the denim circles and secure with epoxy adhesive. On top, add the two fabric petal heads followed by the lace petal head, securing each layer in the center only with adhesive. Allow the flower to dry thoroughly.

7 Turn the flower over. Take a selection of fabric craft leaves, glue them in layers to the back of the flower, and then add the other denim disc on top. Attach a brooch finding to the back of the flower, using the denim strip and epoxy adhesive.

8 Turn the flower back over again and add a large stone or crystal to the flower center, using plenty of epoxy adhesive. Leave everything to dry thoroughly to make sure all the layers are securely fixed in place.

Use lots of epoxy adhesive to fix the fabric parts together as they will absorb the glue quickly, but make sure no adhesive will show on the very front of the flower when it is finished.

Allow each layer to dry thoroughly before fixing the next, both to avoid the flower getting sticky and to prevent previous layers from shifting out of position.

BONES BRACELET

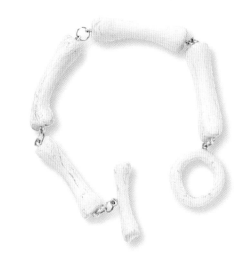

This is one of my favorite pieces in the book—it is really quite straightforward to make and the epoxy putty gives a really tactile, smooth, ceramic finish if sanded well. I recommend making more bones than you intend using, all in different sizes and shapes, so you will have the right combination to make the correct length. Any extra bones could be drilled at one end only and made into a matching pendant or a pair of earrings.

YOU WILL NEED
Materials: *White 2-part epoxy putty, 16-gauge (1.2mm) wire, epoxy adhesive, jump rings*
Tools: *Several grades of emery paper, drill/multi-tool, round-nose pliers, 2 pairs of flat-nose pliers, wire snips*

1 Mix the two parts of the epoxy putty together thoroughly, carefully following the manufacturer's instructions. Mold part of the putty by hand into four bone shapes, making them all slightly different.

2 Make a smaller bone as a T-bar and a bone ring to act as the catch. The small bone needs to pass easily through the ring but be long enough to hold in place. Leave all the bones to dry overnight.

3 Sand all the bones thoroughly all around to even out any small bumps or roughness in the surface and create a very smooth, chalky finish. Work through the grades of emery paper up to around 1200 grit.

4 With the bone clamped in a vice, drill a hole roughly ¼in (5mm) deep in both ends of each of the larger bones. Drill a shallower hole in the center of the small bone on one side, and in the outer edge of the ring.

5 Use the wire to make ten wire eye loops (see page 22) to implant into the epoxy putty. After shaping, cut the stem of the wire down to around ¼in (5mm) each time.

6 Glue the stem of each eye loop into the pre-drilled holes in the bones, using a dab of epoxy adhesive to secure.

7 When the adhesive is fully dry, connect the bones using jump rings, with the small bone at one end and the bone ring on the other side.

LACE BOW HAIR PIN

A quick and lightweight design to create, this black lace pin is adaptable to other fabrics. With a different catch on the reverse it could be worn as a brooch instead, or used to customize a bag. Mixing chain and fabric is an interesting combination and you can hang pretty much anything you choose from the chain lengths.

YOU WILL NEED

Materials: *Lace, narrow velvet ribbon, epoxy adhesive, hair clip finding, oxidized chain, oxidized jump rings, 3 crystal drops, 3 eye pins, flat-backed pearl bead*

Tools: *Fabric scissors, needle and black thread, wire snips, round-nose pliers, 2 pairs of flat-nose pliers*

1 Cut a length of lace around 2in (5cm) wide and long enough to form a large bow. Take a similar length of narrow velvet ribbon and tie another bow to sit on top of the lace one. Glue the bows together in the center.

2 Cut a short strip of the velvet ribbon. Turn the bow over and add a hair clip finding to the back by wrapping the strip of ribbon around the center of the combined bows and the clip, with the ends joining at the back.

3 Glue the ends of the strip of ribbon in place to secure the hair clip finding firmly. Leave the adhesive to dry for the recommended time and then stitch each end of the clip finding to the back layer only of the lace bow, making sure that the stitches will not show on the front.

4 Cut three different short lengths of chain and add to a jump ring. Thread a crystal drop onto an eye pin, create a loop in the stem, and then wrap the end back around the stem to secure, snipping off any excess. Repeat for the other two drops and then attach one to the end of each chain length using a small jump ring.

5 Thread a large jump ring through the center vertical loop of the ribbon bow and to this add the jump ring holding the three beaded chain lengths. To finish, glue a flat-backed pearl bead to the center of the bow.

PADLOCK PENDANT

*I*f you have an old padlock with a missing key lying around, here is the perfect opportunity to make use of it. I recommend that you don't use a very large padlock, though, because this will increase the weight of the pendant quite a lot. Any color/style of ribbon and trim can be used to cover and hang this design, so experiment with what you have available.

YOU WILL NEED
Materials: *Small padlock, waxed cotton cord, epoxy adhesive or superglue, lace/velvet ribbon trim, black enamel paint, satin ribbon, flat-backed crystals, jump rings, key charm, 2 crimp ends, catch, velvet ribbon*
Tools: *Fabric scissors, paintbrush, 2 pairs of flat-nose pliers*

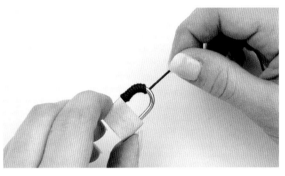

1 To wrap the padlock loop with cotton cord begin by knotting and securing the end with adhesive and then wind the cord neatly around the loop, leaving no gaps. Knot at the other side to finish and glue in place.

2 Cover the body of the padlock with a strip of velvet/lace ribbon trim, securing it in place with adhesive. Cut the trim to fit after it is attached for a neat join with ends that align.

3 Paint the remaining visible metal ends of the padlock carefully with black enamel paint. Add a second coat if required, leaving the paint to dry thoroughly after each coat.

4 Tie a small bow in satin ribbon and glue on a few crystals. Fix the bow to the padlock with adhesive—it is best to position the ribbon so that it covers the join in the trim.

5 Add a jump ring to the center vertical loop of the bow. Add a small key charm to the jump ring before closing.

6 Cut a length of velvet ribbon to the required necklace length and attach it to the top of the padlock with a lark's head knot (see page 30). Add crimp ends to the ends of the ribbon (see page 31). Add the catch to the crimp ends using jump rings.

INSECTS WEB NECKLACE

*T*his piece is best approached when you have time to spare; it's pretty easy but the insects are quite detailed so maybe allow a couple of hours to complete the project. The netting is used in millinery to create fascinators and is readily available in notions (haberdashery) stores.

YOU WILL NEED
Materials: Fimo® Special Effects in various colors, 20-gauge (0.8mm) silver-plated and nylon color coated wire, epoxy adhesive, Fimo® gloss varnish, length of black millinery netting, 2 eye pins, 2 cone crimp ends, jump rings, extension chain, catch
Tools: Wire snips, round-nose pliers, 2 pairs of flat-nose pliers, paintbrush, fabric scissors, needle and black thread
Extra: Fimo® or clay modeling tools

1 Model small Fimo® insects in your chosen colors. Poke small holes in the body for adding wire legs later and a hole into the head to take a hanging loop. Make around 25 insects, then bake in the oven following the manufacturer's instructions. Allow to cool.

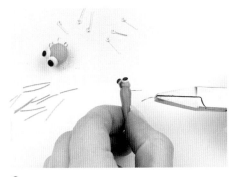

2 Cut small lengths of colored wire for the insect legs. Make an eye loop (see page 22) for each in silver wire, leaving a short stem to insert into the insect body. Glue the legs and an eye loop into the body of each insect using epoxy adhesive. You can paint the insects with gloss varnish if you prefer a shiny effect.

3 Construct the necklace by rolling the netting into a loose tube and gathering the ends together, to form a cylinder that is tight at the ends and spans out centrally. Stitch the ends in place and then stitch loosely along the length of the netting to secure the shape.

4 Thread an eye pin into the narrow end of each cone crimp end, bending the stem over inside to secure. Add adhesive to the ends of the netting cylinder and feed one end into each cone crimp end. Secure the netting and eye pins in the cone crimp end by compressing with pliers, nipping the cones quite tightly.

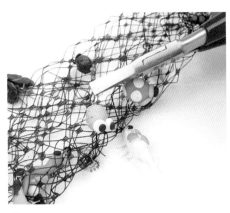

5 Add the Fimo® insects randomly around the netting, using jump rings threaded through the netting and the eye loop in the head of each insect.

6 Using jump rings, add the catch and the length of extension chain to the eye pin loops on the cone end caps.

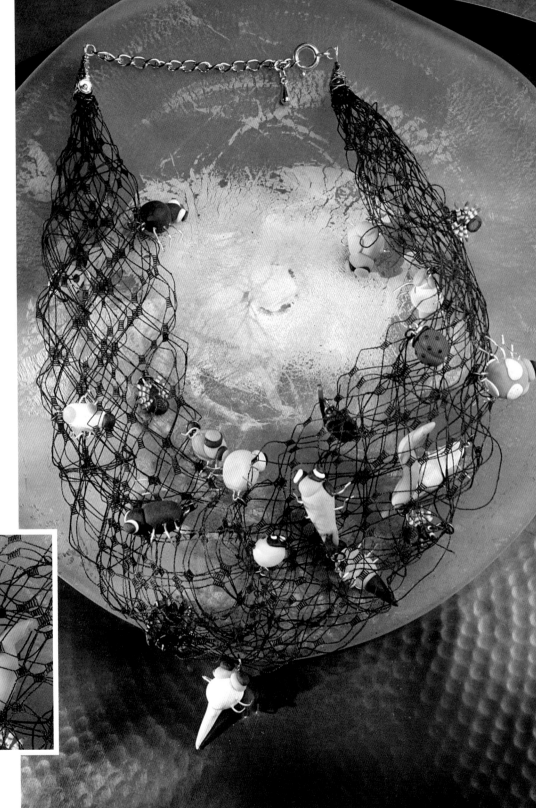

FEATHERED EARRINGS

*T*hese are statement earrings for sure: they are long but hang over your shoulder nicely and move well. I found the bamboo hoops in a bead shop and sprayed them black. An alternative could be wood curtain rod rings, which are a similar size.

YOU WILL NEED

Materials: *2 bamboo hoops, black enamel spray paint, 24-gauge (0.6mm) wire, epoxy adhesive, 2 eye pins, 2 cone end caps, bundle of small feathers, 4 long fine feathers, 4 cord end caps, 2 ear wires, jump rings, short lengths of silver and oxidized color chain, crucifix charms, spike charms*

Tools: *Vice, soft cloth, drill/multi-tool, round-nose pliers, 2 pairs of flat-nose pliers, wire snips*

1 Spray the two bamboo hoops black, using the enamel spray. Add a second coat if required. Allow the paint to dry thoroughly for the recommended time.

2 Holding the hoop in a vice (protecting the paint finish with a soft cloth) drill four holes halfway through the thickness of each hoop; one hole at the top and the other three at the bottom, spaced evenly apart.

3 Make eight wire eye loops (see page 22), leaving a stem of wire roughly the same length as the holes drilled in the hoops in step 2. Glue the eye loops into the drilled holes using a little epoxy adhesive.

4 Thread an eye pin into the smaller end of a cone end cap and cut off any excess stem. Gather the smaller feathers into two small bundles (one for each earring). Position the quill ends together and glue into the wider end of the end cone, using plenty of adhesive.

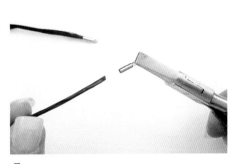

5 Select four similar longer feathers (two for each earring). Add epoxy adhesive to the quill end and glue one into each cord end cap.

6 Add an ear wire to the top eye loop in the bamboo hoop, using a jump ring. Repeat for the other bamboo hoop.

7 Add one of the feather bundles made in step 4 to each earring by connecting the eye loop on the cone end cap to the center eye loop in the bottom of each bamboo hoop, using jump rings. Add two long feathers to an eye loop on one side of each bamboo hoop in the same way.

8 Cut two lengths of silver chain and two of oxidized colored chain. Add the spike and crucifix charms randomly to the chain lengths, using jump rings. Use a jump ring to connect one length of each chain to the final eye loop in each bamboo hoop.

When the glued small feather bundles have dried, very gently pull at the feathers to remove any that have not stuck securely into the cone end.

Clean away excess adhesive with tissue when wet; remove any that you missed with acetone when it's dry.

Remember to mirror the position of the long feathers and chains on each hoop to make a pair of earrings.

CHAPTER 3

METAL WORK, BEADING, & CONSTRUCTION

Projects in this chapter vary in difficulty; I suggest you start with simple construction pieces such as the Vampire Earrings or Jewel Beetle Earrings. Once you are more accustomed to saw piercing and using a multi-tool, the Sweeney Todd Earrings or the Crystal Skull Ring will encourage you to develop your own designs.

SPIDER WEB RING

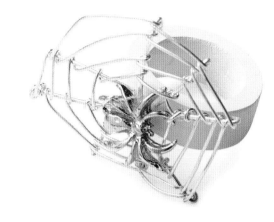

*T*he ring shank in this piece is made of 2-part epoxy putty, the web is silver-plated wire, and the metal spider came from a bead shop. The combination of materials is quite lightweight and the shank feels really smooth when worn. You could vary the color and scale of the piece by constructing your own spider in wire or Fimo®.

YOU WILL NEED
Materials: *White 2-part epoxy putty, 24-gauge (0.6mm) and 20-gauge (0.8mm) silver-plated wire, spider bead, superglue*
Tools: *Wire snips, round- and needle-nose pliers, sandpaper, drill/multi-tool*

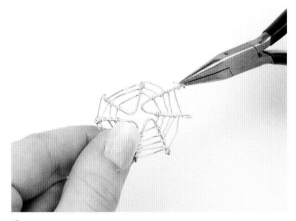

1 Work the epoxy putty in your hands until it is pliable and then roll it into a tube and create a ring-shaped band. Press the band against a clean work surface to create flat edges. Put aside to dry.

2 While the band is drying, start constructing the web. Make four U-shaped lengths in 0.8mm wire and position as shown. Cut around 12in (30cm) of 0.6mm wire and, with the U-shaped parts gripped as positioned, begin wrapping the wire around the "spokes," working over, under, and around each time in a web pattern.

3 Follow the circular web pattern, using needle-nose pliers to secure tight joints and intersections. Once you have wrapped enough rings around the web and are happy with the form (irregular shapes in this case look better), snip any excess wire away. Use pliers to secure the wire ends by bending them back around.

4 Take the dry ring shank and sand all the edges and surfaces smooth and even; wrap sandpaper around a pen or similar cylindrical shape to sand the inside. Smooth one area on the side of the ring shank to create a flat face to take the web.

5 With the ring shank held securely in a vice, carefully drill two small holes right through the flat face created in step 4, spacing the holes around ¼in (5mm) apart.

6 Position the web on top of the shank, add a little superglue to the spider, and place this on top of the web. Make sure the holes in the shank are not concealed.

The 2-part epoxy putty ring shank can also be painted to achieve a different effect. It is better not to use colored Fimo®, because it does not give the same smooth finish.

The thickness of the wire is not critical— you just need two different thicknesses that are easy to shape.

7 Cut a short length of 0.6mm wire, curve it to a U-shape with round-nose pliers, and feed it up through the holes drilled into the shank.

8 On the topside of the ring, use the needle-nose pliers to help secure the web and spider by wrapping the wire ends around both and into the web design to finish.

ANGEL WINGS NECKLACE

Perhaps one of the softer designs in the book, this necklace is easy and inexpensive to make and super light to wear. I like its simplicity, and another reason you should give it a try is that it's very wearable with pretty much anything really.

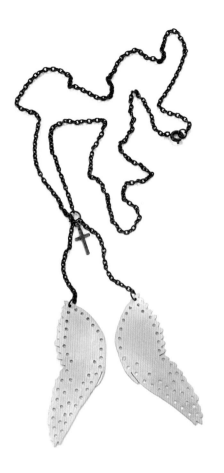

YOU WILL NEED
Materials: *Thin aluminum (or silver) sheet, length of silver chain, jump rings, cross charm, bolt ring catch, liver of sulfur*
Tools: *Piercing saw, file, drill/multi-tool, wire snips, 2 pairs of flat-nose pliers, brass brush*

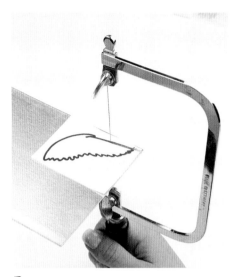

1 Using the template on page 122, cut two wings from thin sheet aluminum or your preferred sheet metal. File any rough edges smooth as necessary.

2 Drill small holes in a random design around the wing edge, continuing up to the tip. Cut a long length of silver chain and add a jump ring in the center. Cut two shorter lengths of chain and hang these from the central jump ring.

3 Add a cross charm to the central jump ring. Add a bolt ring catch and jump ring to the ends of the longer chain and a jump ring to the end of each of the shorter chains. Oxidize everything in liver of sulfur (see page 26).

4 Brush over the surfaces of the two wings using a brass brush. Attach one wing to the end of each of the shorter chains, using flat-nose pliers to open and close the jump rings (see page 22).

ANATOMICAL HEART BROOCH

I *like the idea that some people won't necessarily recognize this form at first.
Using liver of sulfur to oxidize the metal gives a great surface finish that you
can obtain easily at home without any special tools; however, you will have to deal
with a really bad smell from the chemical.*

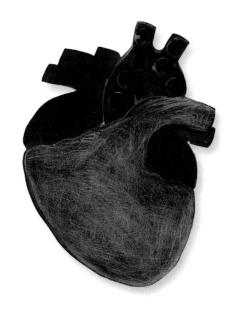

YOU WILL NEED
Materials: *0.5mm copper sheet,
epoxy adhesive, liver of sulfur,
small flat-backed crystals,
large brooch back finding,
renaissance wax*
Tools: *Marker pen, piercing
saw, needle files, coarse emery
paper, soft polishing cloth*

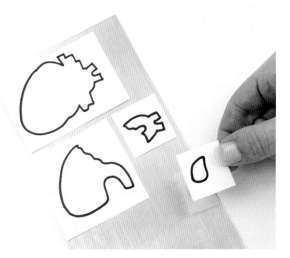

I Copy the templates on page 124 onto the
copper sheet and cut out the shapes with
the piercing saw, as described on page 24.
Use needle files on the edges to smooth out
any irregularities (see page 24).

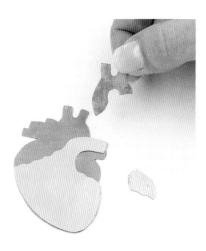

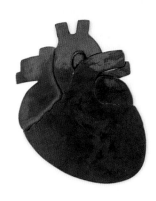

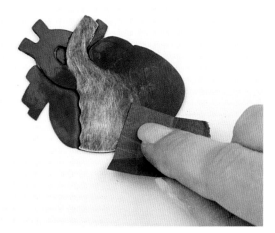

2 Glue the two layers of the heart together
as shown in the photograph, using epoxy
adhesive. Allow the adhesive to dry fully for
the recommended time.

3 Mix a liver of sulfur solution as
explained on page 26. Submerge
the heart in the solution to
oxidize it and add patina.

4 Use coarse emery paper to carefully sand back part of
the oxidized finish from the top heart layer only, to create
a rough scratchy appearance on this section.

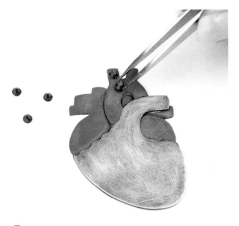

5 Glue the crystals to the pipe of the top heart layer using epoxy adhesive, and then glue the brooch back finding to the reverse of the bottom heart layer.

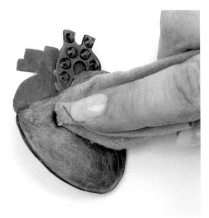

6 Rub a little renaissance wax onto the heart surface to seal the oxidization.

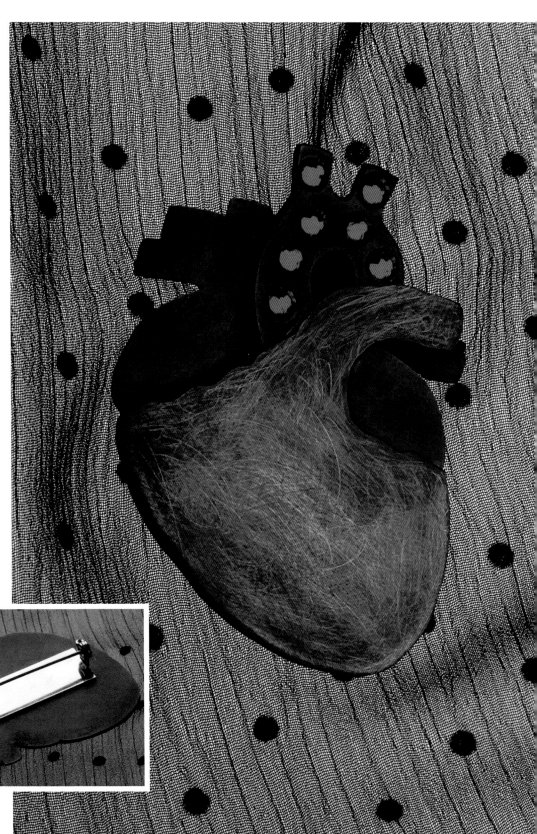

GOTHIC CHANDELIER EARRINGS

*T*hese earrings reflect the style of Phantom of the Opera and although they are quite extravagant in scale, they are not too heavy to wear. They require mainly beading and wire work to construct: some of the threading is a little complicated, but the simple Fimo® joints reduce the amount of wire manipulation needed.

YOU WILL NEED

Materials: *20-gauge (0.8mm) silver-plated wire, 2 ear wires, Fimo® (classic) in black and one other color, 86 large (around 3.5mm) black beads, 0.3mm clear beading thread, epoxy adhesive, 10 crimp beads suitable for 0.3mm beading thread, 300 smaller (around 2mm) black beads, 10 pear-shaped glass beads*

Tools: *Ruler, wire snips, round- and flat-nose pliers, craft knife, pin*

1 Measure out ten 1½in (4cm) lengths of wire and two 3½in (9cm) lengths. Take one of the longer lengths and use round-nose pliers to form a loop at one end. Add an ear wire and then twist the wire around to close the loop. Repeat on the other long wire.

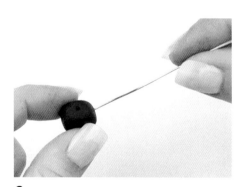

2 Using black Fimo®, form two central balls by rolling between your palms and then flatten the top and base. Take one of the cut wires and use it to make a hole right through the center of both balls. Use the same wire to pierce five equally spaced holes, each around ⅛in (3mm) deep, around the middle of the ball.

3 Make two rounded end cones in black Fimo®. Use the wire to pierce a ⅛in (3mm) deep hole in the flat top side of each cone. Form ten small balls of black Fimo® and almost completely flatten them to make the candle base plates. Pierce each base completely through the center with the wire.

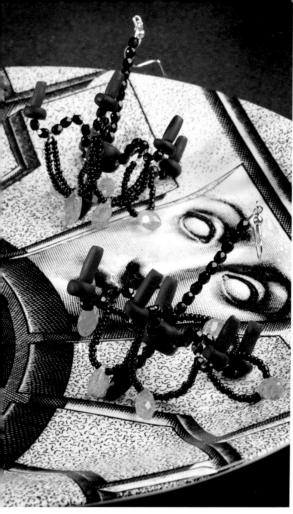

4 For the candles, select another Fimo® color and roll out a cylindrical tube. Use a craft knife to cut ten sections. Use the wire to pierce a hole in the base end of each candle, up to halfway through the length. Bake all the Fimo® parts (two central balls, two end cones, ten base plates, ten candles) following the manufacturer's instructions. Allow to cool.

5 Thread ten of the larger black beads onto one of the stems that is attached to an ear wire. Add one of the central balls made in step 2 and then thread on a further three beads. Snip the excess wire down to just 1/8in (3mm) and insert this into the end cone, using a little epoxy adhesive to secure.

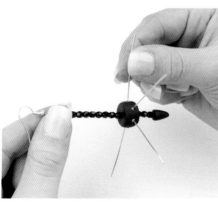

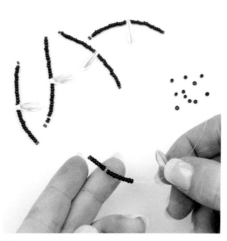

6 Take five of the shorter wire lengths and apply epoxy adhesive to one end of each. Insert into the five holes around the central ball. Support these wire arms with props as needed and allow to dry completely.

7 Cut a length of beading thread and use the flat-nose pliers and a crimp bead to add a loop to one end (see page 31). Thread on 15 small round beads and then add one of the pear-shaped crystals. Add a further 15 small beads and then finish with another loop. Make another four drapes the same.

8 Thread around four of the larger beads onto each wire arm of the chandelier and then add the loop end of two of the drapes to each arm, so that the drapes will hang between the arms. Add a further two large beads to each arm.

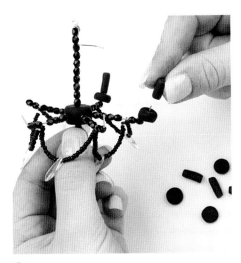

9 Glue a base plate and then a candle to the end of each wire arm, trimming excess wire as before but allowing a little extra length for flexibility when bending the arms. The arms can be partially bent at this stage to support the candlesticks in an upright drying position. Repeat steps 5–9 for the other earring.

10 Leave the chandeliers overnight—or at least for several hours—before shaping the arms. It is easiest to manipulate the wire by hand, but pliers may also be used gently to help achieve awkward undulations.

This project uses silver-plated wire, which is an affordable alternative to pure silver wire. The silvery color will be maintained providing you store the wire in a sealed bag when you are not working on it to prevent exposure to air or the damp.

When using the epoxy adhesive to fit wire ends or other small parts, the best method I have found is to dip a pin or toothpick into the mixed glue and insert this into the hole before adding the part to be fixed. Alternatively, dip the wire end into the epoxy adhesive.

JEWEL BEETLE EARRINGS

I purchased the beetle shells on eBay, but I have also seen them on Internet craft sites. They are not expensive and they generally come with a pre-drilled hole through the top. When making the "pods" that conceal the pearls, pick shells that pair together well.

YOU WILL NEED

Materials: *8 or more white and dark pearl beads, 8 head pins, jump rings, 16 jewel beetle shells in matching pairs, 2 ear wires, length of oxidized chain*
Tools: *Round-nose pliers, 2 pairs of flat-nose pliers, wire snips*

1 Thread a pearl onto a head pin and then make an eye loop in the stem (see page 22), snipping away any excess wire. Create eight of these pearl dangles—you can vary the type of pearl you use and add two pearls to a few of the head pins.

2 Take a jump ring and thread on one beetle shell followed by the loop end of a pearl dangle. Add another beetle shell to the jump ring before closing, to form a "pod" around the pearl. Make eight pods like this in total.

3 Cut four lengths of chain, each a different length. Use a jump ring to add these to an ear wire. Cut four more lengths to match the first set and add to the second ear wire so that you have a matching pair.

4 Add one beetle shell and pearl pod to the end of each of the lengths of chain using jump rings. Repeat for the other earring.

SWEENEY TODD EARRINGS

I *would definitely wear these, either as a pair or individually. You will need patience to make the meat cleaver, but it's not as tricky as it might look—and I guarantee you'll be really pleased with the result. I used silver for a super-shiny surface, but it's fine to use thick aluminum sheet if you're on a budget.*

YOU WILL NEED

Materials: *Silver or aluminum sheet metal, square walnut rod, epoxy adhesive, brass rod, brass tubing, 24-gauge (0.6mm) gauge silver-plated wire, 2 ear wires, jump rings, gloss varnish, red teardrop glass bead*

Tools: *Piercing saw, files, emery paper, brass brush, drill/multi-tool, vice, parallel pliers, bench block, hammer, wire snips, round-nose pliers, 2 pairs of flat-nose pliers, burnisher, paintbrush*

1 Use the templates provided on page 124 to cut the razor blade and the meat cleaver blade from the sheet silver or aluminum.

2 Carefully file and sand the edges of all the metal parts to remove any rough edges. Use a brass brush to brighten up the flat surfaces on both pieces.

3 Cut a short length of walnut rod for the cleaver handle. Use the multi-tool with a sanding drum bit to round the end like a handle. Tidy by hand with a file.

4 Clamp the handle in a vice and cut down a little way to remove a slice the thickness of the metal to house the blade. Fit the blade into the handle, using a little epoxy adhesive to secure.

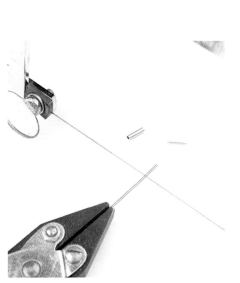

5 Drill three holes spaced along the cleaver handle to fit the outside diameter of your rod and tubing. One of the holes should be positioned so that it will pass through the blade as well.

6 Grip the brass rod or tubing using parallel pliers—this will help when cutting short lengths. Cut two lengths of rod and one of tubing, each ¹⁄₁₆in (1.5mm) longer than the thickness of your handle.

7 Position the length of tubing in the end hole in the handle and the two rods in the other two holes. Place on a bench block or hard surface and hammer to flatten the ends like rivets (see page 25).

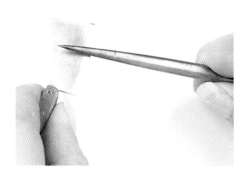

8 Create a U-shaped wire hook and bend the end of each arm inward. Tuck one bent end into the tubing rivet in the knife handle and then squeeze the U-hook slightly so that the other bent end clips into the other side of the handle. Connect the cleaver to an ear wire using a jump ring.

9 Work on the edge of the cleaver blade with a burnisher to define the cutting edge of the blade and to make it look as if it has been sharpened. Add some gloss varnish or wax to the walnut cleaver handle to finish.

10 Drill the razor blade at one end to attach a jump ring and an ear wire. Add the teardrop red glass bead to the other end, using a jump ring through the base of the shaped slot in the center of the blade.

BARBED WIRE BRACELET

*T*his angry-looking bracelet is relatively quick to make, especially if you are able to find flexible aluminum wire in your local craft supplies store. The colors used here are optional—if you would prefer a more masculine effect, try using only silver-colored wire. Another striking combination is black cord with gold wire barbs.

YOU WILL NEED
Materials: Silver or colored flexible aluminum wire, waxed black cord
Tools: Circular former, 2 pairs of flat-nose pliers, wire snips, fabric scissors

1 Use a paintbrush or pen as a former to create the coils. Take the flexible aluminum wire and wrap it two or three times around the former, using pliers to pull the wire tight, and then snip the coil off, leaving spiked ends. Repeat to create around 20 coiled barbs. If you have trouble gripping the wire as well as the former, try gripping the former in a vice. This will free both hands for the wrapping process, so that you can keep the coils tight to one another.

2 Make the end coils for the T-bar catch in the same way, but use larger items to wrap around. One end coil must be able to pass through the other; the ends of the spikes can be straightened out to stop the catch from pulling back out when worn.

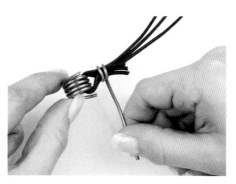

3 Cut three lengths of black cord at least 2in (5cm) longer than your wrist size. Take all three cord ends through one end coil and back on themselves to form a loop. To secure the loop in place, take another short length of wire and wrap it tightly around the cords.

4 Thread the coiled barbs loosely onto the cord bracelet, allowing a little extra space for comfort of movement. Add the other end coil in the same way as in step 3, tightly securing the cord loop in place with one last wire wrap.

SECRET BOTTLE PENDANT

*F*inding a small bottle for this design shouldn't be a problem—good choices
could include empty spice bottles or a perfume atomizer. As with the padlock
pendant (page 50), it is advisable to keep the scale fairly small, otherwise the
necklace will be heavy to wear.

YOU WILL NEED
Materials: *Small lightweight
glass bottle with lid, 20-gauge
(0.8mm) wire, Fimo®
Classic in black, 2 wing
beads, epoxy adhesive, narrow
red ribbon, 2 crimp ends,
jump rings, catch, key charm,
imitation blood, narrow
black suede ribbon*
Tools: *Drill/multi-tool, wire
snips, round-nose pliers,
fabric scissors, 2 pairs of
flat-nose pliers*

1 Drill two holes a short way apart into the
top of the lid of the small bottle. Make a
U-shaped bail from wire and glue the ends
into the holes in the lid to secure firmly in
place. Make two small Fimo® stoppers to hold
the wing beads, then push them against the
sides of the bottle lid to ensure a good fit.

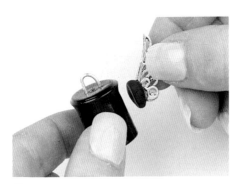

2 Separate the Fimo® stoppers from the lid
and remove the wing beads. Bake the Fimo®
to harden, following the manufacturer's
instructions, and allow to cool. Glue the wing
beads into the stoppers using epoxy adhesive.
Allow to dry thoroughly and then glue a wing
assembly to each side of the bottle lid.

3 Cut a length of ribbon to suit your required
length of necklace and attach it to the bail on
the top of the bottle using a lark's head knot
(see page 30). Finish the ribbon ends with
crimp ends (see page 31) and add a catch
using jump rings (see page 23). Put the key
charm into the bottle and fill it up with
imitation blood.

4 Replace the cap on the bottle—add a little
adhesive beforehand to secure it firmly in place
if necessary, particularly if it is a push-on lid
and not a screw top. Tie a small bow in the
black suede ribbon and glue this to the front
of the bottle lid.

NUT AND CHAIN NECKLACE

*T*he chain I used for this necklace—and the Bell Chain Bracelet on page 84—was from a hardware store. You can purchase larger, thicker chains from these types of outlets and they tend to cut by the yard/meter. The gold charm findings were my own selection from a bead shop, but you can use whatever you prefer.

YOU WILL NEED
Materials: *Large-linked black chain, flat black suede cord, waxed black cotton cord, assorted gold charms (crucifix, bells) and beads, black nuts, jump rings, 2 lengths of black satin ribbon, superglue, large bolt ring catch*
Tools: *Wire snips, scissors, 2 pairs of flat-nose pliers*

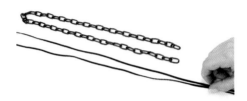

1 Cut a length of chain for your desired length of necklace. Measure out a length of suede and a length of cotton cord, each 2–4in (5–10cm) longer than the full length of the chain.

2 Add beads/charms/nuts to the suede cord at random intervals. Use knots on either side to stop the beads from traveling along the cord length. Repeat using the cotton cord.

3 Cut both cords down if necessary so that they match the length of the chain, allowing a little extra at each end for knotting. Knot both the cords neatly to the last link in the chain at each end. Add a large jump ring to each end of the chain.

4 Feed a length of black satin ribbon through the last chain links at one end. Gather the chain and cords together and wrap the ribbon neatly around to secure. Knot the ends of the ribbon together and finish with a bow. Repeat on the other side.

5 Add a little adhesive to the wrapped ribbon/bows to secure; epoxy or fabric glue is fine. Attach a large bolt ring catch to the ends of the chain using jump rings. Add a few additional charms along the chain at random, using jump rings.

BELL CHAIN BRACELET

A matching accessory to the long Nut and Chain Necklace on page 82, this bracelet is very simple to make—it just needs part assembly. For a very different look, you could try using a lighter weight or an alternative color of chain.

YOU WILL NEED
Materials: *Large-linked black chain, jump rings, small bell charms, large bolt ring catch*
Tools: *Wire snips, 2 pairs of flat-nose pliers*

1 Wrap a double length of chain loosely around your wrist, allowing a little extra for twisting. Cut the chain to this length.

2 Fold the length of the chain in half and twist the two strands together loosely. Secure the twist in place, using jump rings at intervals along the length.

3 Add bell charms to the chain links at random, using jump rings. Add a large bolt ring catch to the chain ends, using jump rings.

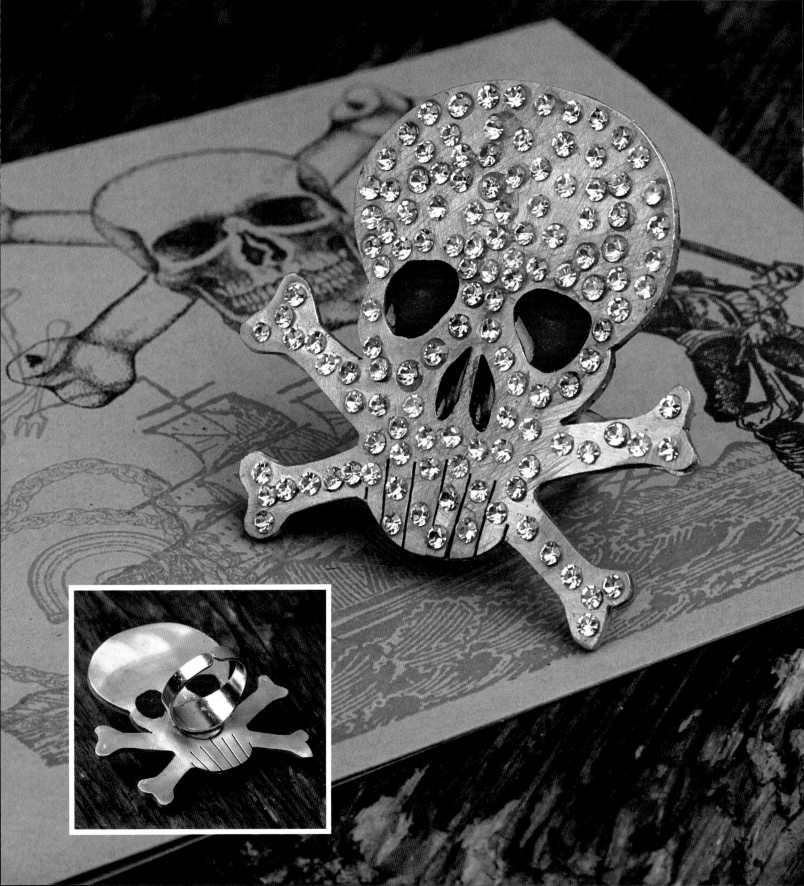

CRYSTAL SKULL RING

*T*he skull and crossbones motif is a well-known warning symbol and this ring is a big and bold representation of it. The design combines cubic zircon crystals and colored resin, which interact with the light. Like many designs in this book, the skull can be made as a pendant instead by drilling a hole through the top and adding a jump ring.

YOU WILL NEED

Materials: *1mm aluminum sheet, cubic zircon faceted crystals, epoxy adhesive, superglue, ring shank finding, adhesive tape, casting resin, coloring pigments*

Tools: *Piercing saw, drill/multi-tool, files, emery paper, tweezers, pin, needle file*

1 Using the templates on page 123, mark out two skull shapes on the sheet of aluminum. Cut out the shapes with a piercing saw. Drill a hole to access the internal spaces with your saw blade (see page 25).

2 Take the top skull (with the mouth) and drill holes all across it at random. The holes should be large enough to fit the crystals without the stones falling through.

3 File and sand both skulls smooth, finishing with emery paper. Glue the crystals into the drilled holes in the top skull, using tweezers and a little epoxy adhesive applied with the tip of a pin.

4 Glue the skulls together with superglue and attach a shank finding to the back. When fully dry, file and sand around the edges so they line up neatly. Apply tape behind the eyes to create a surface to set resin over. Mix colored resin according to the manufacturer's instructions (see page 27); you only need a tiny quantity.

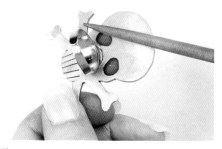

5 Add the resin and leave the ring overnight to dry, positioning it so that the resin can dry flat to the surface. When it is fully dry, remove the plastic tape from the back and carefully file away any escaped resin using a needle file.

"ARGHHH" NECKLACE

I wear a "HARI" text necklace in this horror poster style font all the time. The template for "Arghhh" is provided, but why not also experiment writing your own name or a different word in this font style? You could also cut this design from acrylic sheet instead of using copper, or you could use any metal sheet that you prefer.

YOU WILL NEED
Materials: *0.5mm copper sheet, 2 lengths of oxidized chain, jump rings, catch, knife charm, resin with red pigment*
Tools: *Piercing saw, drill/multi-tool, files, emery paper, brass brush, 2 pairs of flat-nose pliers*

1 Use the template on page 122 to mark out "Arghhh" on your copper sheet. Saw pierce out the shape, using a drill to access the internal details (see page 25).

2 File and sand the edges of the lettering to smooth and pick out the fine detailing. Go over the metal surface with a brass brush to "frost" the finish.

3 Drill a small hole in the top of the text on each side. Attach a length of chain on each side, using jump rings. Use two more jump rings to add a catch at the back of the chain.

4 Add a knife charm (or cut one yourself from the copper sheet) as a subtle detail, using a jump ring through the chain near the catch of the necklace. For an even more gruesome effect, dip the knife in a little red resin for a blood-coated look.

Hang heavier/larger charms on the longest chain lengths to ensure the weighting is balanced.

If you cannot find charms you like, try making your own; the spikes could be copied in Fimo® and any shape could be cut from sheet wood or metal.

VAMPIRE EARRINGS

*B*asically an assembly project, this is perhaps one for filling a spare 20 minutes sometime. You could make the crosses yourself from square wood rod, as I did for the crucifix bracelet—just scale them down a little so they are not too heavy for earrings.

YOU WILL NEED
Materials: *Length of white colored chain, jump rings, 2 ear wires, eye pins, 2 wood cross beads, wire, 2 red pear-shaped glass beads, 2 gold spike beads, 2 shark's tooth beads*
Tools: *Wire snips, 2 pairs of flat-nose pliers*

1 Cut three different lengths of chain and then cut another three to match. Connect each set of three to an ear wire using jump rings.

2 Make two bead dangles, using two of the eye pins and the two wood cross beads (see page 23). Add eye pins to the other beads in the same way, if required.

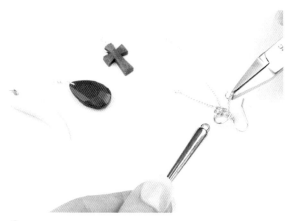

3 Add a cross dangle, a red bead, and a spike bead to each earring, fixing one to the end of each chain using jump rings. Add a shark's tooth bead to the jump ring at the base of each ear wire.

GOTHIC CROSS NECKLACE

*A*nother traditional Gothic design for the Dracula fans out there. Quite a few different materials went into making this cross but don't let that put you off as it is very simple to construct. You can change the specific combination of crystals/ribbon/beads to suit what you can find, or to match your preferences.

YOU WILL NEED
Materials: *3mm walnut sheet, 0.5mm copper sheet, selection of flat-backed crystals, liver of sulfur, 20-gauge (0.8mm) silver-plated wire, epoxy adhesive, renaissance wax, cord, spacer bead, selection of silver-toned beads, thin black cord, crimp beads, velvet ribbon, crimp ends, jump rings, catch, chain extension*
Tools: *Marker pen, piercing saw, drill/multi-tool, files, emery paper, brass brush, round-nose pliers, 2 pairs of flat-nose pliers*

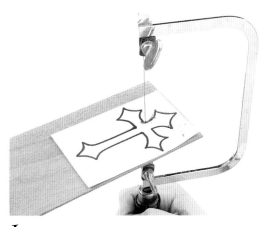

1 Use the cross template on page 123 to mark out one cross on the walnut sheet and one on the copper. Cut both crosses out using a piercing saw.

2 Using the template for guidance, mark the position of the holes on the copper sheet with a marker pen. Drill holes through the sheet large enough to fit the crystals.

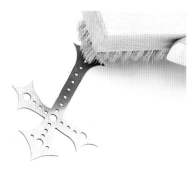

3 File the copper cross to tidy the edges and then oxidize it in liver of sulfur solution (see page 26). Brush the surface finish back with a brass brush to give a caviar-color effect.

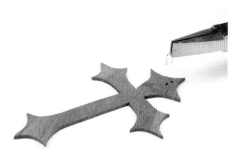

4 Sand the walnut cross smooth and then drill two small holes into the back at the top. Make a U-shaped bail in 0.8mm wire and glue this into the holes in the back of the cross.

5 Glue the copper cross onto the front of the walnut cross using epoxy adhesive. Glue the crystals into the holes in the copper cross.

6 File the cross edges carefully with a needle file to ensure they align—this will also remove the oxidized coloration to brighten up the copper edges. Rub some renaissance wax onto the surface of the copper cross.

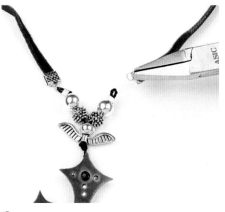

7 Thread a length of thin cord through the bail on the back of the walnut cross. Knot and add a spacer bead (I used a wing bead), then thread a matching sequence of silver-toned beads onto each side. Loop the excess cord at each end after the beads, using a crimp bead (see page 31). Trim off any excess cord.

8 Cut two lengths of velvet ribbon to the approximate length you want your necklace and add crimp ends to each end of both ribbons (see page 31). Use a jump ring to link a crimp end onto the cord loop on each side of the cross assembly.

9 At the back of the necklace add the catch to the other ribbon ends using jump rings. You can also use a chain extension to allow for some flexibility in the wearing size.

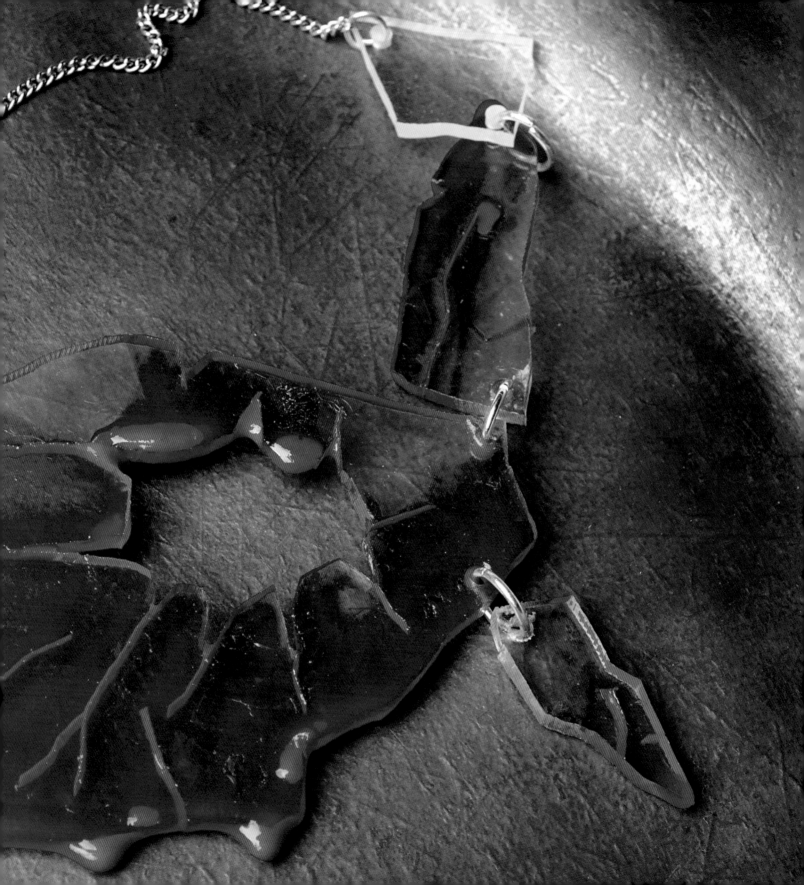

CHAPTER 4

ACRYLIC, RESIN, & WOOD

This chapter introduces alternative sheet materials from which to
pierce out flat forms. I use walnut wood sheet and rod for its depth
of color and relative durability, while acrylic sheet or colored resin
bring interest and variation to your jewelry and look great in
combination with different metal tones.

CRUCIFIX BRACELET

Y*ou will need some square wood rod to make this bracelet—I found quite a large selection in a model-making supply store and opted for walnut due to its strength and deep color. The beads are wooden ones from a bead store and are threaded onto the same waxed brown cotton cord as that wrapped around the cross.*

YOU WILL NEED
Materials: Walnut square rod, epoxy adhesive, waxed brown cotton cord, 12–14 assorted wooden beads, crimp ends, jump rings, bolt ring catch
Tools: Piercing saw, files, emery paper, drill/multi tool, fabric scissors, 2 pairs of flat-nose pliers

1 Cut one long and two short sections of walnut rod to form a cross. Sand the edges straight and glue together as shown above, using epoxy adhesive. Set aside to dry and then sand again to remove any escaped adhesive.

2 Drill a hole from side to side through the top arm of the cross. Wrap a length of cord several times around the center of the cross, as shown above. Knot the ends neatly to secure and trim off any excess cord.

3 Cut a length of cord to fit your wrist, allowing a little extra for ease of wear. Thread on the cross and then add half the wooden beads onto each side.

4 Add a crimp end to each end of the cord as described on page 31. To finish, use jump rings to add the bolt ring catch to the crimp ends.

CORD CHARM BRACELET

*T*his project has a nice range of materials: leather, wood, metal, and plastic—but these are all used in many other projects in this book so don't be put off. The main technique required is saw piercing shapes from sheet to create the charms, which are then hung from the leather cord using jump rings.

YOU WILL NEED
Materials: *3mm black acrylic sheet, 1mm aluminum sheet, walnut wood sheet, leather cord, jump rings, 2 beads that thread snugly onto the cord, epoxy adhesive*
Tools: *Piercing saw, files, emery paper, drill/multi-tool, 2 pairs of flat-nose pliers*

1 Copy the Bat template on page 122 onto the protective cover of the acrylic sheet and use the piercing saw to cut out the shape (see page 24). Remove the protective coverings and sand the edges and the surface of the acrylic to frost. Drill a hole near the top.

2 Copy the Skull template on page 122 onto the aluminum sheet. Cut out the shape, drilling holes to access the internal areas (see page 25). To create a scratched surface finish, use a coarse brush in the electric multi-tool. Drill a hole near the top.

3 Copy the Coffin template on page 122 onto the walnut wood sheet and cut out with the piercing saw, drilling a hole to access the cross. File and sand the edges as required to smooth any rough areas. Drill a hole near the top edge.

4 Cut a length of leather cord around 4in (10cm) longer than the circumference of your wrist. Use a pair of sliding knots to join on the two ends (see page 30).

5 Use jump rings to add each charm to the cord. Cut any excess cord away after the knots and glue a bead to each end using a little epoxy adhesive. Allow to dry.

BAT BROOCH

A fun piece with a real sense of movement! Using a heat gun will allow you to manipulate the flat plastic form to create curves easily. The edges of the acrylic can be polished up really well to give a high shine and the red crystal eyes will sparkle in the light.

YOU WILL NEED

Materials: *3mm black acrylic sheet, oxidized chain, jump rings, flat-backed red crystals, superglue, brooch finding*

Tools: *Piercing saw, drill/multi-tool, files, emery paper, heat gun, 2 pairs of flat-nose pliers*

Extra: *Protective gloves*

1 Transfer the Bat template on page 123 onto the protective cover of the acrylic sheet. Use a piercing saw to cut out the shape. Drill a small hole near a point on the wing at either side.

2 File and sand the acrylic edges to smooth all the marks away (see page 24). Remove the protective coverings. Using a heat gun, apply even heat over the whole bat form until the acrylic becomes soft and flexible.

3 Wearing thick protective gloves, shape the acrylic to mirror the bat form as shown. Keep the back flat so that the brooch pin can be fitted. Hold in place to maintain the shape until the acrylic cools and sets.

4 Cut two different short lengths of oxidized chain and hang these from the drilled holes in the bat wings using jump rings. Glue the red crystal eyes to the front face and the brooch finding to the center back.

Do not overheat the acrylic, as it will bubble and spoil. Apply heat gradually; if you are unhappy with the form, allow the piece to cool and then heat up again to reshape.

To cool and set the acrylic quickly, quench under running water.

SHATTERED GLASS NECKLACE

*H*ere the jagged edges of shattered glass are recreated in clear (far less *dangerous!*) acrylic sheet, a material that is straightforward to use but gives a professional finished result. The addition of red resin "blood" is an optional extra for a more gory finish!

YOU WILL NEED
Materials: 3mm clear acrylic sheet, large jump rings, length of chain, bolt ring catch
Tools: Marker pen, piercing saw + extra blades, drill/multi-tool, files, wet-and-dry emery paper, 2 pairs of flat-nose pliers, wire snips
Extra: Resin with red pigment, resin mixing equipment

1 Use a marker pen to draw out some shard pieces on the protective cover of the acrylic sheet. These shapes can really be random and irregular. Using a piercing saw, cut around the marked outline to create the jagged shapes.

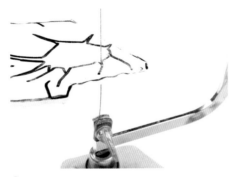

2 Mark a hole at either side of each shape in a suitable position to link the pieces together and drill the holes through. Drill a hole in the center of the large shard to access the internal detail to be sawn out (see page 25).

3 Use files to begin smoothing all the cut edges (see page 24). To remove final scratches from the cut edges, use wet-and-dry emery paper with water and sand smooth, working in the same direction all the time (see page 24).

4 Link the parts together using jump rings. Cut two pieces of chain the desired length of the necklace and attach to the end acrylic pieces with jump rings. Add a bolt ring catch to the ends of the chain using jump rings.

Do not remove the protective coverings from your acrylic sheet until you finish all the filing work. Acrylic is easily scratched and the flat surface cannot be sanded to remove markings—unless you want the entire surface to have a frosted appearance.

5 If you want the gory effect, before fixing the acrylic shapes together dip one or more into red casting resin (see page 27). Add the resin sparingly, tilting the shape gradually to allow excess to flow off but avoiding drips. You may find it difficult to control this, as the resin is very runny. Set aside to dry flat before using.

VELVET AND PEARL CUFF

*T*his is quite an elaborate cuff, but a good opportunity to become confident using a heat gun on acrylic sheet. Once you are comfortable forming plastic this way, you will be able to create your own bangle and ring designs. Threading the suede cord through the holes is a lengthy process, but it finishes the edge off really successfully.

YOU WILL NEED
Materials: *3mm red acrylic sheet, wide velvet ribbon, epoxy adhesive, flat-backed pearl beads, flat suede cord, superglue*
Tools: *Piercing saw, drill/multi-tool, files, wet-and-dry emery paper, heat gun, tweezers*
Extra: *Protective gloves*

1 Cut a rectangle around 2 x 6¾in (5 x 17cm) from acrylic sheet. Drill equally spaced holes all the way around the edge at least ½in (1cm) apart and large enough to thread the suede cord through.

2 File the edges of the acrylic sheet working in one direction only, following the marks on the plastic edge (see page 24). Finish the edges off with wet-and-dry emery paper, using a little water. Remove the protective coverings when you have finished.

3 Heat the plastic with a heat gun (see page 29) until it begins to soften. Wearing protective gloves, form the acrylic into the cuff bangle shape—this is a trial-and-error process and you may need to alter the form a number of times to fit.

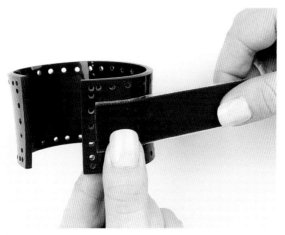

4 After shaping, allow the cuff to cool completely. Cut a length of velvet ribbon just a little shorter than the length of the cuff, so that it fits inside the drilled holes. Glue the ribbon around the center using a little epoxy adhesive.

5 Using the epoxy adhesive again, glue the flat-backed pearls in a row down either side of the ribbon, using tweezers to place them accurately. Be careful not to cover up any of the drilled holes.

6 Allow the adhesive to dry thoroughly and then take a long length of suede cord and thread it through one corner hole on the cuff. Tie a small, tight knot on the underside to secure the end. Begin weaving the thread in and out of the holes to create a stitched pattern around the cuff.

7 Finish at the hole next to where you started with another knot. Trim off any excess cord and add a dab of superglue to the knots to secure.

Heat forming the bangle to a symmetrical form that also fits well is difficult and will probably take a few alterations. Allow to cool and then slowly heat again to adapt isolated areas.

8 Make two small bows from short lengths of the suede cord. Glue a bow to each end of the cuff as shown in the photograph on the right, on alternate corners.

SCREW EARRINGS

A fun pair of earrings to make and people won't understand how you got the screws inside! The resin parts could be used for various jewelry applications: you could hang one from a chain as a pendant, or for a ring you would just need to attach a shank finding to the back face.

YOU WILL NEED

Materials: *Small screws and nuts, casting resin, 2 ear wires, jump rings, 24-gauge (0.6mm) silver-plated wire, epoxy adhesive*

Tools: *Mold tray, resin mixing equipment, 2 pairs of flat-nose pliers, emery paper, vice, drill/multi-tool, wire snips, round-nose pliers*

1 Find a pair of appropriate molds to take your selection of screws—you don't have to use the same shape or size as those shown here. Position the screws as you would like them to sit and fill the two molds with casting resin (see page 27), following the manufacturer's instructions. Set the resin aside to dry for the recommended time.

You can experiment with different combinations and styles of nuts/bolts/screws in this design and change the effect further by mixing a little translucent colored pigment to the resin.

2 Take the pair of ear wires and hang a small nut from each using a jump ring. Add a second jump ring to the bottom of each nut to take the cast resin shapes later.

3 Remove the resin shapes from the molds and sand the edges smooth if necessary. Place the shapes in a vice and carefully drill a hole around ¼in (5mm) deep in the top of each.

4 Make two wire eye loops (see page 22) with stems around ¼in (5mm). Dip each stem into epoxy adhesive and insert into the drilled holes. When fully dry, connect a resin shape to each earring using the jump ring at the base.

TOMBSTONE NECKLACE

*T*his is a pretty glitzy tombstone as tombstones go... I made the front face black, but there's no reason why it couldn't be pink for an even more ironic look! The flower beads are ready-made Fimo® ones, which I found in a bead store, but you could make your own.

YOU WILL NEED

Materials: *3mm sheet acrylic sheet in red and black, epoxy adhesive, resin with white pigment, small flat-backed crystals, jump rings, oxidized chain, flower beads, eye pins, leaf beads, bolt ring catch*

Tools: *Piercing saw, drill/multi-tool, files, emery paper, resin measuring equipment, tweezers, 2 pairs of flat-nose pliers, round-nose pliers, wire snips*

1 Copy the templates on page 124 onto the protective cover of the acrylic sheet and cut out with a piercing saw. Cut the "cracks" and cut out the text (see page 24) on one shape. Keep the tiny pieces cut out from the top half-round of the R and P to replace later. Remove the protective coverings and stick the layers together with epoxy adhesive.

2 When the adhesive is completely dry, file and sand around the edges of the tombstone to ensure the layers match up perfectly. Lightly sand across the top surface, using fine emery paper to give a frosted effect. Drill two holes through all layers, one on each side near the top for hanging.

3 Replace the tiny pieces cut from the center of the R and the P. Mix resin with white pigment (see page 27) and add sparingly to the text and tombstone cracks. When completely dry, sand any escaped or excess resin away if necessary. Add crystals to the tombstone face using epoxy adhesive.

4 Use jump rings to attach a length of chain to each side of the tombstone. Create flower bead links by threading an eye pin through the bead, and then bending the stem on the other side into a matching eye loop (see page 22). Snip away any excess stem. Make as many as you like—I have used eight in this example.

5 Cut the chain with snips at regular intervals and insert a flower bead link by partially opening the eye loop on either side and closing again when connected. Add the catch with jump rings. I found some matching Fimo® leaf charms in a bead shop, so I also added these to the flowers using jump rings.

BOTTLE TOP CAMEO BRACELET

Recycling is always a good idea, so this bracelet is practical as well as fun. You get to have a few drinks first, too—so it's win win really! Use whatever charms you like to fill the cameos—and remember that changing the color you spray the bottle tops and the pigment color for the resin can change the look totally.

YOU WILL NEED
Materials: *Around 5 soda/beer bottle tops, enamel spray paint, 20-gauge (0.8mm) silver-plated wire, bead charms (skulls and flowers), superglue, resin with black pigment, jump rings, bolt ring catch*

Tools: *Drill/multi-tool, wire snips, round-nose pliers, resin mixing equipment, 2 pairs of flat-nose pliers*

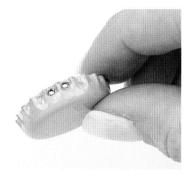

1 Drill two holes quite close together through either side of each bottle top. Spray each top with enamel spray paint—you may need several coats for dark-colored tops.

Experiment with the number of bottle tops you need to circle your wrist before starting—a standard bottle top is roughly 1in (2.5cm) in diameter and you can measure your wrist with a tape measure.

2 Use round-nose pliers to make two U-shaped hooks for each bottle cap, so that the ends will fit into the drilled holes. Place in position—they will be secured in place when the resin is added.

3 Position one of your chosen beads centrally inside each top—you can superglue to secure if necessary. Fill around each bead with resin (see page 27), stopping before the beads are submerged. Set aside to dry.

4 Connect the tops together with jump rings through the U-shaped hooks at the sides— I used two rings per connection for durability. Add a bolt ring catch; you could also add an extension chain for a variable fit.

BOTTLE TOP CAMEO RING & EARRINGS

*T*he making process here is pretty similar to that required for the cameo bracelet project (see page 115): more recycling and more drinks—soft ones, of course! Making the bottle caps into brooch pins would also be a great twist on a standard round badge—just add a brooch finding to the back instead of shank/ear studs.

YOU WILL NEED

Materials: Soda/beer bottle tops, enamel spray paint, bead/charm or found item for each top, superglue, resin with color pigment of choice, ring shank finding, ear stud findings, epoxy adhesive
Tools: Resin mixing equipment

1 Spray all the bottle tops with enamel spray paint, adding extra coats to cover completely as required. Set aside and allow to dry for the recommended time.

Using objects you find lying around at home or out and about can add originality to a piece of jewelry— and obviously keep costs down.

2 Glue one of the bead/charm/found objects centrally within each top. Mix the resin with a colored pigment of your choice (see page 27), following the manufacturer's instructions.

3 Pour the resin carefully into each bottle top around the object to be set. You could also drop some crystals or small beads in while the resin is still wet.

4 Set the bottle tops aside so that the resin can dry for the manufacturer's recommended time. Turn the tops over and glue on your ring shank or a pair of ear stud backs.

AMBER SPIDER NECKLACE

*A*nother favorite of mine... try your local joke shop or novelty store for a selection of bugs—you should also find some imitation blood there for the Secret Bottle Pendant on page 80. The resin with amber pigment really glows under light, so this piece is eye catching for many reasons!

YOU WILL NEED

Materials: Plastic insect, resin with amber pigment, 20-gauge (0.8mm) and 24-gauge (0.6mm) silver-plated wire, jump rings, chain, catch

Tools: Mold tray, resin mixing equipment, files, emery paper, drill/multi-tool, round-nose pliers, wire snips, 2 pairs of flat-nose pliers

1 Position your chosen plastic insect inside the mold. Mix the resin with amber pigment (see page 27) and pour over the insect—this necklace uses six "amber" beads, but you can make more or fewer; they do not all need to be the same size or shape.

You can set any insect you like in this design—your best bet is to look in a joke shop, novelty store, or science museum for a good selection. Alternatively you could use a real insect if it's dry—the resin will seal it just as real amber does.

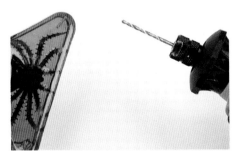

2 Leave the resin to dry completely for the manufacturer's recommended time. Carefully remove the shapes from the tray and tidy up any rough edges with a file or emery paper (see page 24). Drill a ¼in (5mm) deep hole into either end of each shape.

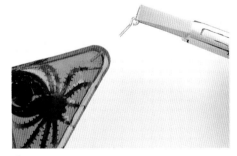

3 Make two wire eye loops for the largest bead from 0.8mm wire (see page 22). For the smaller beads use 0.6mm wire, with the ends wrapped around the stem for extra interest. Leave a stem of around ¼in (5mm) on each eye loop to insert into the drilled holes in the resin. Secure with epoxy adhesive.

4 Use jump rings to connect the beads together in a suitable sequence and then add a length of chain to the final bead on either side to make the necklace the length you require. Attach a catch of your choice at the back.

PENTAGRAM RING

Making this design requires a little extra concentration to ensure a good result: the techniques are not too difficult—you will have used them many times in this book already—but you need a steady hand to saw the shapes accurately. Any sheet metal could be used for this piece, or acrylic sheet if you prefer.

YOU WILL NEED
Materials: *1mm and 1.5mm aluminum (or silver) sheet, epoxy adhesive, resin with red and black pigment, metal polish, ring shank finding*
Tools: *Piercing saw, drill/multi-tool, needle files, resin mixing equipment, emery paper, polishing cloth*

1 Copy the template on page 124 onto the thinner metal sheet. Cut out the shape with the piercing saw, drilling the star to access internal areas (see page 24). Take your time sawing this shape, because irregularities will be noticeable—it is best to saw outside the line and file back to straighten afterward as necessary.

2 Use needle files to finish the shape, tidying up any detailing. Glue the shape to the thicker sheet of aluminum, using epoxy adhesive. When the adhesive is dry, cut out around the outer edge only with the piercing saw. File the edges to align perfectly.

3 Mix a small amount of resin with the red pigment (see page 27). Pour a tiny amount into the outside areas of the star. Leave to dry for the manufacturer's recommended time. Mix the black resin as before and fill the internal areas. Leave to dry for the recommended time again.

4 When all the resin is completely dry, sand over the surface with wet emery paper to remove any excess resin. Shine the surface with metal polish and a soft cloth. To finish, add a ring shank finding to the back of the disc, using epoxy adhesive.

TEMPLATES

Angel Wings Necklace (page 64)

"Arghhh" Necklace (page 88)

Cord Charm Bracelet (page 100)

Crystal Skull Ring (page 87)

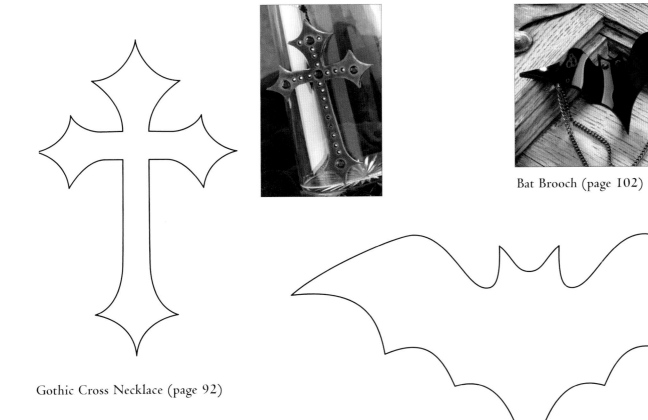

Gothic Cross Necklace (page 92)

Bat Brooch (page 102)

Anatomical Heart Brooch (page 66)

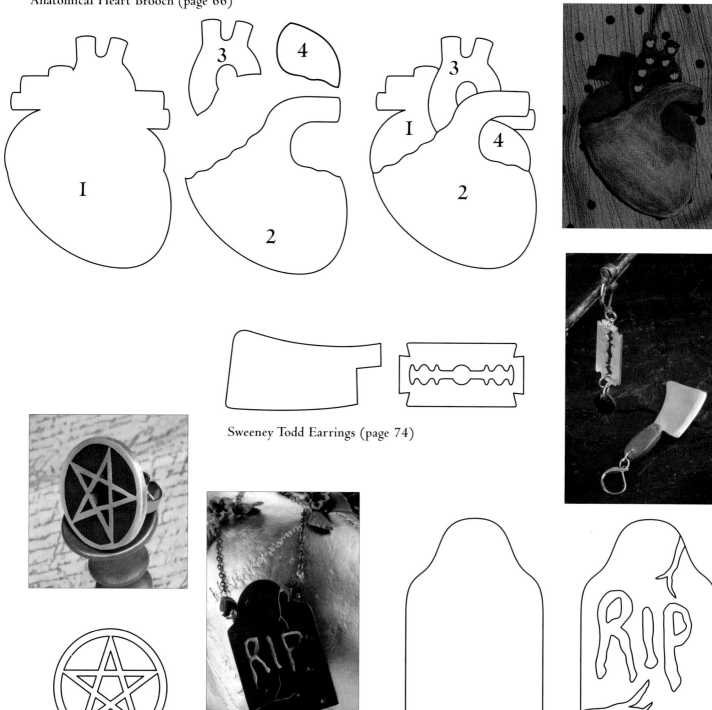

Sweeney Todd Earrings (page 74)

Pentagram Ring (page 120)   Tombstone Necklace (page 112)

SUPPLIERS

INTERNET RESOURCES

Harriet Smith
www.harihorror.com

Rio Grande
www.riogrande.com
Comprehensive selection of jewelry-making
tools and materials

Fire Mountain Gems and Beads
www.firemountaingems.com
Beads, crystals, findings, tools, stringing
materials, mold-making equipment, sculpting
materials

Beadaholique
www.beadaholique.com
Comprehensive selection of beads, findings,
stringing materials, tools

Beadworks
www.beadworks.com
Beads, findings, and stringing materials

Beaducation
www.beaducation.com
Beads, findings, stringing materials, tools

Beadalon, Inc.
www.beadalon.com
Basic jewelry findings, stringing materials

www.findingtools.com
Comprehensive selection of tools and adhesives

National Jewelers Supplies
www.nationaljewelerssupplies.com
Comprehensive selection of jewelry-making
tools

Art Supplies Online
800-967-7367
www.artsuppliesonline.com

Envirotex
www.eti-usa.com
Casting resin

www.metalclay.co.uk
Tools, molds, ready-made findings

www.beadsandcrystals.co.uk
Swarovski HotFix crystals, beads

www.e-beads.co.uk
Beads, findings

www.i-beads.eu
Beads, findings

Swarovski Crystallized Stores
London/New York/Shanghai/Austria
www.swarovski-crystallized.com
Full range of HotFix crystals, other crystals

NORTH AMERICA

Art, craft, and model making

Jo-ann Fabric & Crafts
Stores nationwide
www.joann.com

Jewelry-making supplies

Hobby Lobby Stores
Stores nationwide
www.hobbylobby.com
Comprehensive selection of jewelry-making
tools and materials

Michaels Stores
Stores nationwide
1800-642-4235
www.michaels.com
Tools, beads, findings, stringing materials

Out on a Whim
121 E. Cotali Avenue
Cotati
CA 94931
www.whimbeads.com
Tools, beads, findings, wire, stringing materials

Beads, findings, stringing materials

Atlanta Bead Company
North American General Offices
781 Wheeler Street, Studio 18
Atlanta
GA 30318
www.atlantabeadcompany.com

The Beadin' Path
15 Main Street
Freeport
ME 04032
www.beadinpath.com
Beads, findings, stringing materials

Bead It!
590 Farrington Highway
Kapolei
HI 96707
www.ibeads.com
Beads, findings, wire, stringing materials

Sheet metal

K& S Engineering
www.ksmetals.com
Copper, brass, aluminum

Ace Hardware
www.acehardware.com
Specialty nuts, bolts, copper sheeting, pipe

Continued overleaf

UNITED KINGDOM

Art, craft, and model making

4D Modelshop
The Arches
120 Leman Street
London E1 8EU
www.modelshop.co.uk
Vast selection of sheet materials, rod, tubing,
mold-making/casting materials

London Graphic Centre
Three stores in central London
www.londongraphics.co.uk
Mold-making materials, resin, acrylic sheet,
polymer clay

Cass Art London
Five stores in central London
www.cassart.co.uk
Polymer clay and paints

Beads, wire, and findings

Bead Aura Ltd
3 Neal's Yard
London WC2H 9DP
www.beadaura.co.uk
Beads, stringing materials

Beadworks
21a Tower Street
Covent Garden
London WC2H 9NS
www.beadworks.co.uk
Beads, findings, stringing materials

The London Beadshop
24 Earlham Street
London WC2H 9LN
www.londonbeadshop.co.uk
Large selection of beads

Scientific Wire Company
18 Raven Road
London E18 1HW
www.wires.co.uk
All types of wire for jewelry making

Bellore
39 Greville St
London EC1N 8PJ
www.bellore.co.uk
Precious metal findings, chain, stones, tools

The Bead Shop (Edinburgh)
6 Dean Park Street
Stockbridge
Edinburgh EH4 1JW
www.beadshopscotland.co.uk
Beads, crystals

The Bead Shop (Nottingham)
7 Market Street
Nottingham NG1 6HY
www.mailorderbeads.co.uk
Beads, crystals

Jencel
www.jencel.co.uk
Beads, findings

Sewing materials

Kleins
5 Noel St
London W1F 8GD
www.kleins.co.uk
Specialist sewing notions, ribbons

Borovick Fabric Ltd
16 Berwick St
London W1F 0HP
www.borovickfabricsltd.co.uk
Good selection of unusual fabrics

MacCulloch & Wallis
25–26 Dering Street
London W1S 1AT
www.macculloch-wallis.co.uk
Sewing notions, trimmings, threads

John Lewis
Stores nationwide
www.johnlewis.com
Excellent sewing notions in larger stores, fabric

Jeweler's supplies

Cooksons
London/Birmingham jewelry quarters
www.cooksongold.com
Precious metals, jeweler's tools

Walsh
London/Beckenham/Birmingham
www.hswalsh.com
Tools, chemicals

Plastics and heat guns

Alec Tiranti Ltd
27 Warren St
London W1T 5NB
www.tiranti.co.uk
Casting resin, mold-making materials

Hamar Acrylic Fabrications Ltd
238–240 Bethnal Green Road
London E2 0AA
www.hamaracrylic.co.uk
Sheet acrylic cut to size

Maplin
Stores nationwide
www.maplin.co.uk
Electronic specialist, heat guns

INDEX

Acknowledgments

A big thank you to Cindy Richards for trusting me with this book, and to Dawn Bates and Sally
Powell at Cico for all their help and support. I'd also like to thank Luis Peral-Aranda for his
creative styling and design layout, Martin Norris for his talented photography, Stephen Dew for
drawing up the templates so clearly, and Marie Clayton for her detailed editing.